Spelling
Games and Activities

GRADE 1

All illustrations and photography, including those from Shutterstock.com, are protected by copyright.

Writing: Tiffany Hailey
Content Editing: Kathleen Jorgensen
Lisa Vitarisi Mathews
Copy Editing: Laurie Westrich
Art Direction: Yuki Meyer
Illustration: Mary Rojas
Cover Design: Yuki Meyer
Design/Production: Paula Acojido
Yuki Meyer
Jessica Onken

EMC 8271
Congratulations on your purchase of some of the finest teaching materials in the world.

Photocopying the pages in this book is permitted for single-classroom use only. Making photocopies for additional classes or schools is prohibited.

For information about other Evan-Moor products, call 1-800-777-4362, fax 1-800-777-4332, or visit our website, www.evan-moor.com. Entire contents © 2023 Evan-Moor Corporation 10 Harris Court, Suite C-3, Monterey, CA 93940-5773. Printed in USA.

Contents

What's in *Spelling Games and Activities* 4

How to Use *Spelling Games and Activities* 7

Spelling Word List 8

Themed Units

Let Your Feelings Show 11
> Words about feelings featuring consonant blends **sc** and **sm** and words ending in **y**

Clean Mouth 21
> Words about teeth featuring consonant digraphs **sh** and **th**; consonant blends **br** and **fl**; and words ending in **y**

In the Kitchen 31
> Words about food featuring words with hard and soft **c**; vowel pairs **ui** and **oo**; and consonant blends **fr**, **sc**, and **sl**

In the Garden 41
> Words about things in a garden featuring **r**-controlled vowels; compound words; and consonant blends **dr**, **fl**, **gr**, and **sp**

Fun at the Fair 51
> Words about the fair featuring consonant blends **fr**, **pr**, **sp**, and **scr** and vowel pairs **ai**, **ea**, **ee**, **ie**, and **oo**

Rainy Days 61
> Words about rain featuring diphthong **ou**; consonant blends **br**, **cl**, **spl**, and **st**; and consonant digraph **sh**

Camping in the Forest 71
> Words about camping in the forest featuring **r**-controlled vowels; compound words; and diphthong **ou**

In the Deep Blue Sea 81
> Words about the sea featuring consonant digraphs **ph**, **sh**, and **wh**; consonant blend **cr**; and compound words

Extra Practice Worksheets 91

Spelling Strategies 152

Answer Key 159

What's in Spelling Games and Activities

Support for Writing
Spelling skills are essential for children to practice in order to communicate well in writing. Many people rely on technology to fix their spelling, but technology can only guess what the writer means. Spelling must be accurate to be understood. Even though there are many spelling rules and even more exceptions, spelling practice can help students understand those rules and apply them to their writing.

Spelling Games and Activities gives you two ways to help your students practice spelling:

- the engaging themed unit section, which brings together related words in grade-appropriate contexts in fun and interesting ways
- the extra practice worksheets section, which uses words from Evan-Moor's *Building Spelling Skills* series and can be used to enrich those lessons or on its own

8 Themed Units
Spelling Games and Activities offers 8 units of grade-level topics that engage students and provide context for practicing spelling useful words. Each unit introduces 8 theme-related words along with the spelling patterns and rules that are used in those words. The unit continues with fun puzzles, cutouts, and other activities to practice writing and spelling the words, followed by a game or other special activity done as a class or in small groups.

Unit Features
You can assign all the pages in a cohesive unit or choose individual worksheets as needed to support your spelling program or to reinforce words learned in other content areas. Each 10-page unit provides a set of spelling words and related spelling tips, a variety of activity pages, and a game or project with teacher directions.

Unit Overview

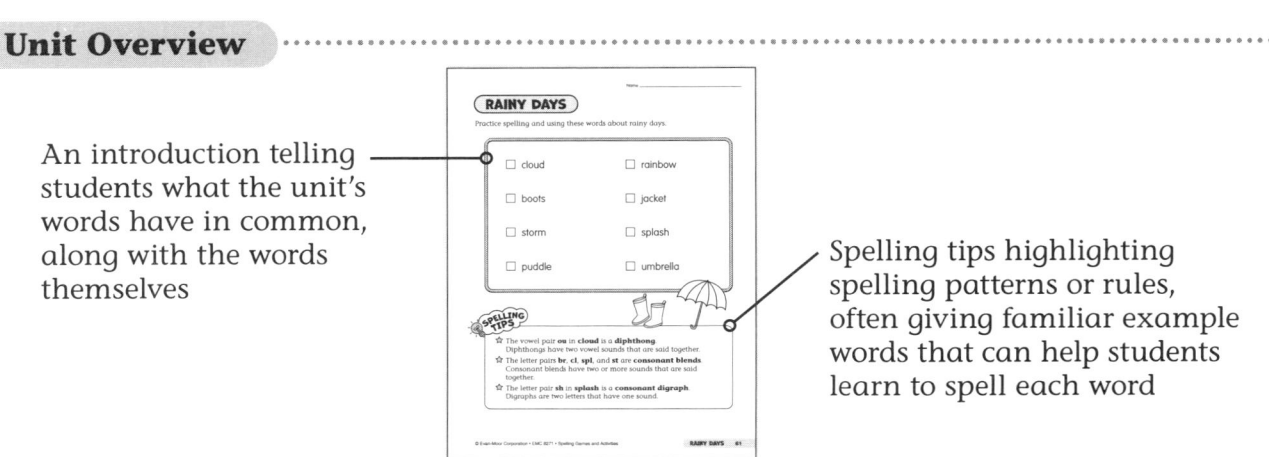

An introduction telling students what the unit's words have in common, along with the words themselves

Spelling tips highlighting spelling patterns or rules, often giving familiar example words that can help students learn to spell each word

What's in Spelling Games and Activities, continued

Theme-Based Activity Pages

There are a wide variety of theme-based activities in every theme unit. These are some examples.

Color spelling patterns
Students look for spelling patterns and color each one using a rule to reveal a picture.

Make a path
Students connect words or follow a maze using spelling patterns to reach the end.

Cut and glue
Students cut and glue letters or pictures to complete or categorize words.

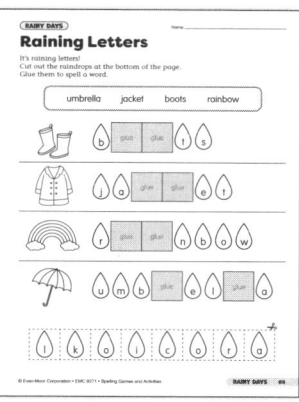

Use rhyme and context clues
Students find and write words that sound right and make sense to complete a rhyme.

Game, Activity, or Hands-on Center

A fun art game, activity, role-play, or other activity lets students practice their words in a small or large group setting.

A page of instructions and materials for the teacher is included.

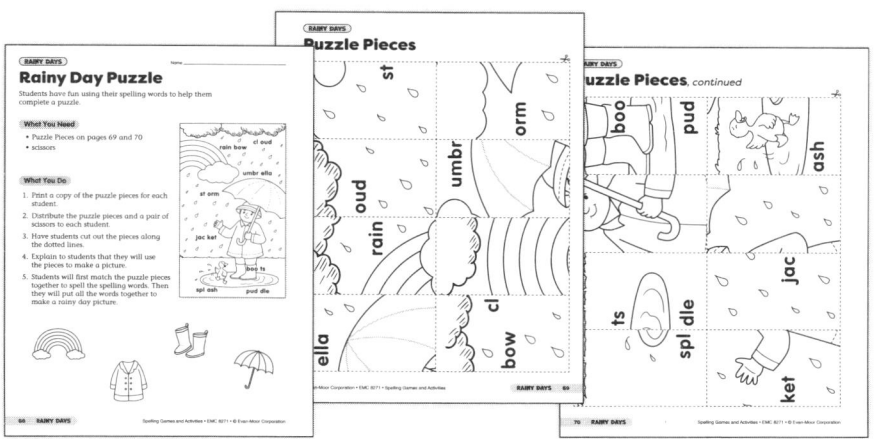

© Evan-Moor Corporation • EMC 8271 • Spelling Games and Activities

What's in Spelling Games and Activities, continued

Extra Practice Worksheets

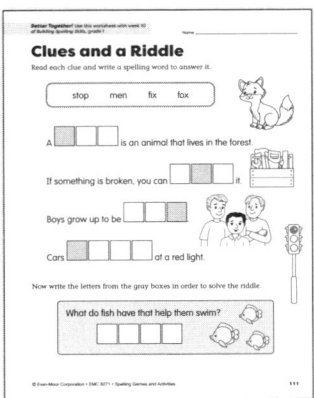  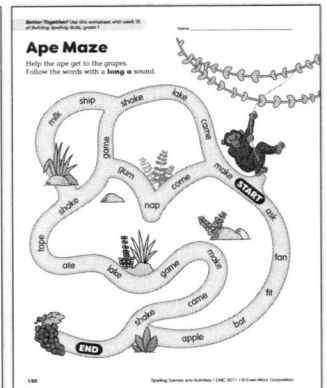

Students apply the same spelling tips from the themed units to sets of words from *Building Spelling Skills*. These pages can be used independently or with any spelling series.

Additional Resources

Spelling Strategies

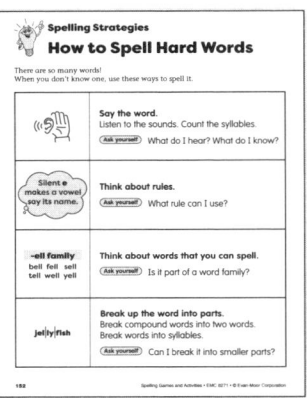 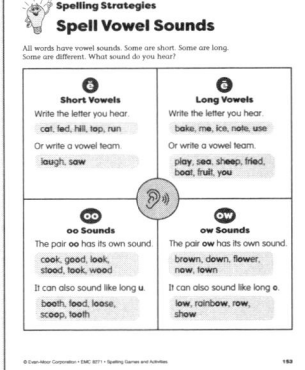 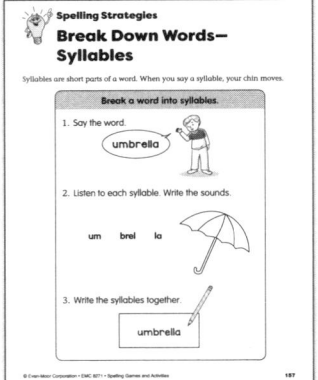

A variety of useful strategies that help students learn a word's spelling by analyzing sounds and word structures or by using dictionary skills and memory aids

Spelling Word List

Alphabetized glossary of all spelling words in the book

Answer Key

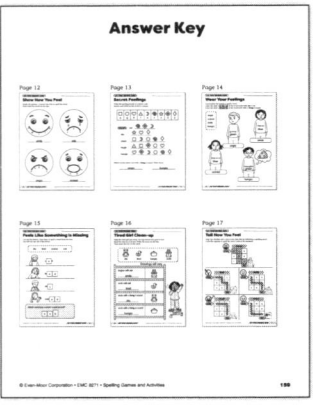

Provided for any page that has student answers. The correct answer or a sample response is shown unless the question is completely open-ended.

How to Use Spelling Games and Activities

Flexible Use

Decide which pages you will use. You can use an entire unit from the themed section, pages focusing on a particular skill, or extra practice pages that apply skills to different words. Then print copies for your students. It is recommended that you include the introduction page that provides helpful spelling tips for the skills you're working on.

Connections to Other Subjects

The units in this book were chosen to represent common experiences of children in first grade, along with general grade-level words. These topics may relate to other subjects you are teaching and could augment other lessons. For example, Let Your Feelings Show could be used with an SEL lesson focusing on managing feelings. Clean Mouth could be used when talking about self-care. In the Garden, Camping in the Forest, or In the Deep Blue Sea could extend a science lesson about plants, animals, or the outdoors. Rainy Days could be used when students must spend recess inside on a rainy day. Use any set of spelling words with a handwriting lesson for extra practice in both.

Extend the Challenge or the Words

If you find an activity or game particularly useful, feel free to use it as a template for other sets of spelling words or other features of the same words. For example, the activity on page 55 asks students to "knock down" cans with words that have a long vowel. You could also ask them to knock down cans with words that start with a blend or have a vowel digraph. You could also change the words on the cans and give students a new target.

Use the Extra Practice Worksheets

If you want additional practice on specific skills or want students to practice applying skills to a new set of words, use pages from the extra practice section. This section features all the spelling words from Evan-Moor's *Building Spelling Skills* weekly lessons. If you are using *Building Spelling Skills*, you can use these extra practice worksheets to enhance your weekly lessons, giving students more practice with the same words.

© Evan-Moor Corporation • EMC 8271 • Spelling Games and Activities

Spelling Word List

a	bell	came	dish
all	bend	can	do
am	big	car	dog
an	bike	cat	dolphin
and	boat	cats	down
angry	bones	cave	dragonfly
ant	book	cavity	fair
are	booth	cloud	fairy
as	boots	coat	fall
at	boxes	come	far
ate	brown	cone	farm
away	brush	cook	fast
backpack	bugs	cow	fawn
bake	bunny	crab	fed
ball	bus	day	feet
be	but	deer	fell
bear	butterfly	did	find
beds	by	dig	fine
bees	cakes	dime	five
beetle	call	dirt	fix

floss	he	last	mouth
flower	hide	late	must
food	hike	laugh	my
forest	hill	law	name
fox	his	lawn	need
foxes	home	let	nest
fried	hot	like	nine
fruit	hungry	line	not
fun	I	little	note
funny	ice	look	now
game	in	loose	octopus
gate	is	low	on
gave	it	make	otter
get	jacket	man	pan
go	jar	may	pat
good	jeep	me	paw
got	jellyfish	men	penny
grasshopper	juice	mind	pet
had	kind	mine	pigs
hand	kites	mitten	play
happy	kitten	mix	prize
harm	ladybug	most	puddle
hat	lake	mountain	pup

puppy	shake	start	tops
put	shark	stay	town
rainbow	she	step	tree
rake	sheep	still	tub
ran	shell	stood	umbrella
red	ship	stop	up
ribbon	show	storm	us
ride	shy	sun	use
rinse	sit	take	wall
robe	six	tape	want
ropes	slice	tell	we
roses	small	ten	well
row	smell	tent	went
run	smile	the	whale
sand	snake	then	what
sat	so	this	wheel
saw	sob	time	will
scared	spider	tired	wish
scoop	spin	to	wood
scream	splash	toad	you
seahorse	stamp	took	
see	stand	tooth	
sent	star	top	

LET YOUR FEELINGS SHOW

Practice spelling and using these words about feelings.

- ☐ angry
- ☐ hungry
- ☐ shy
- ☐ sob

- ☐ tired
- ☐ scared
- ☐ laugh
- ☐ smile

SPELLING TIPS

★ The letter pairs **sc** and **sm** are **consonant blends**. Consonant blends have two sounds that are said together.

★ The letter **y** at the end of a word can have the **long i** sound or the **long e** sound.

LET YOUR FEELINGS SHOW

Name _____

Show How You Feel

Finish the picture. Connect the dots to spell the word.
Then write the word on the line.

_____

_____

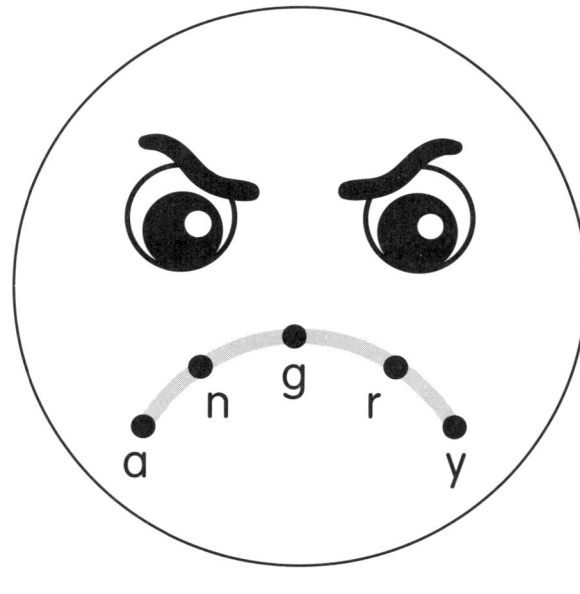

_____

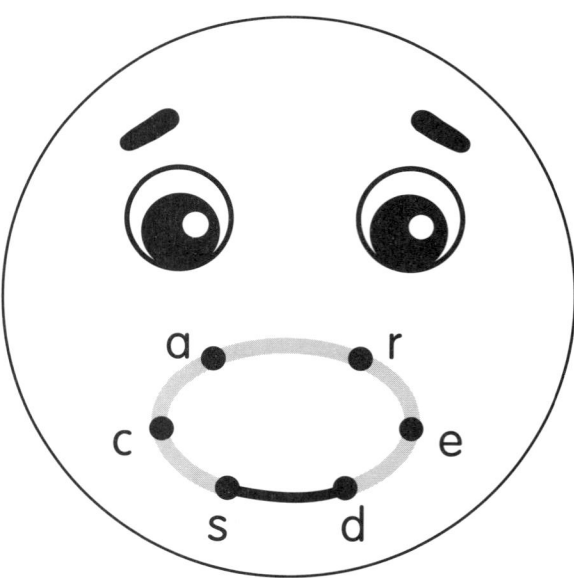

_____

LET YOUR FEELINGS SHOW

Name _____

Secret Feelings

Write the spelling words in a secret code.
Match each letter in the word to a shape.

Example run ____ ____ ____

shy ____ ____ ____

angry ____ ____ ____ ____ ____

laugh ____ ____ ____ ____ ____

hungry ____ ____ ____ ____ ____ ____

Which words above end with a **long e** sound? Write them.

_____   _____

Wear Your Feelings

LET YOUR FEELINGS SHOW

Name _____

Unscramble the letters to spell a word.
Color the shirt 🖍 BLUE if the word starts with **sm** or **sc**.
Color the shirt 🖍 GREEN if the word ends with a **long e** sound.

- angry
- scared
- smile
- hungry

LET YOUR FEELINGS SHOW

Name _____

Feels Like Something Is Missing

Cut out the letters. Glue them to spell a word from the box.
You will not use all of the letters.

shy   tired   scared   sob

s [glue] b

tir [glue] [glue]

sh [glue]

scar [glue] [glue]

Which word has a short vowel sound?

e
y
d
e
o
o
s
y
d
e
b

LET YOUR FEELINGS SHOW

Tired Girl Clean-up

LET YOUR FEELINGS SHOW

Name _____

Help the tired girl put away her toys before she goes to bed.
Read the clue in each row. Write the word on the line.
Then draw the toy on the shelf.

shy   tired   hungry   smile

begins with **sm**

_____

ends with **ed**

_____

ends with a **long i** sound

_____

ends with a **long e** sound

_____

Tell How You Feel

LET YOUR FEELINGS SHOW

Name _____

Help the children tell a friend how they feel by following a spelling word. Color the squares to spell the word. Look at the example.

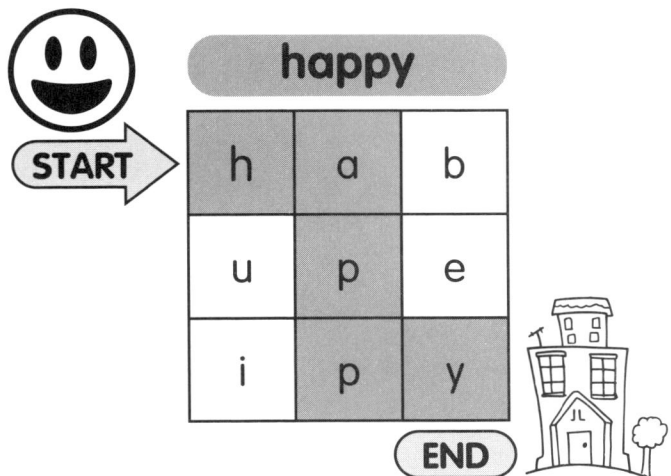

LET YOUR FEELINGS SHOW

Spinning Feelings

Students have fun spelling words using a spinner that shows pictures of feelings.

What You Need

- Feelings Wheel on page 19
- Game Sheet on page 20
- scissors
- paper clip
- pencil

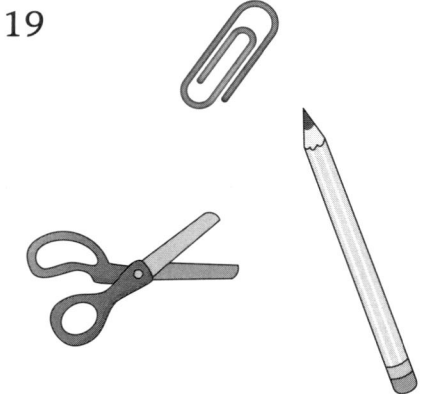

How to Play

1. Print a copy of the Feelings Wheel for each pair of students. Print a copy of the Game Sheet for every student.

2. Cut out the wheel and poke a hole in the center.

3. Show students how to use the spinner. Push a pencil into the center point of the spinner and through the end of the paper clip. Flick the paper clip and watch it spin.

4. Put students into pairs.

5. Distribute two game sheets, a wheel, a paper clip, and a pencil to each pair of students.

6. Explain to students that they will take turns with their partner spelling words that tell about the pictures on the wheel.

7. The first person in each pair spins the paper clip and names the picture that the paper clip lands on. On the game sheet, he or she writes the spelling word that tells about the picture. Then it is the next person's turn to spin the wheel.

8. Have each partner spin the wheel 4 times.

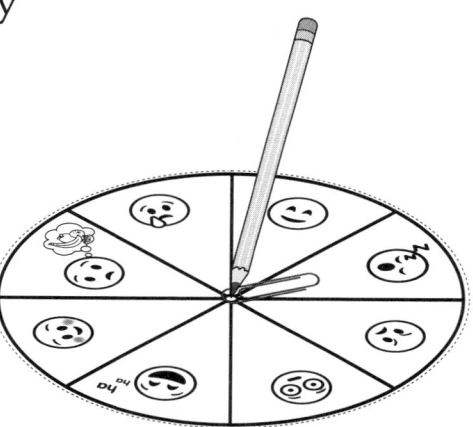

LET YOUR FEELINGS SHOW

Feelings Wheel

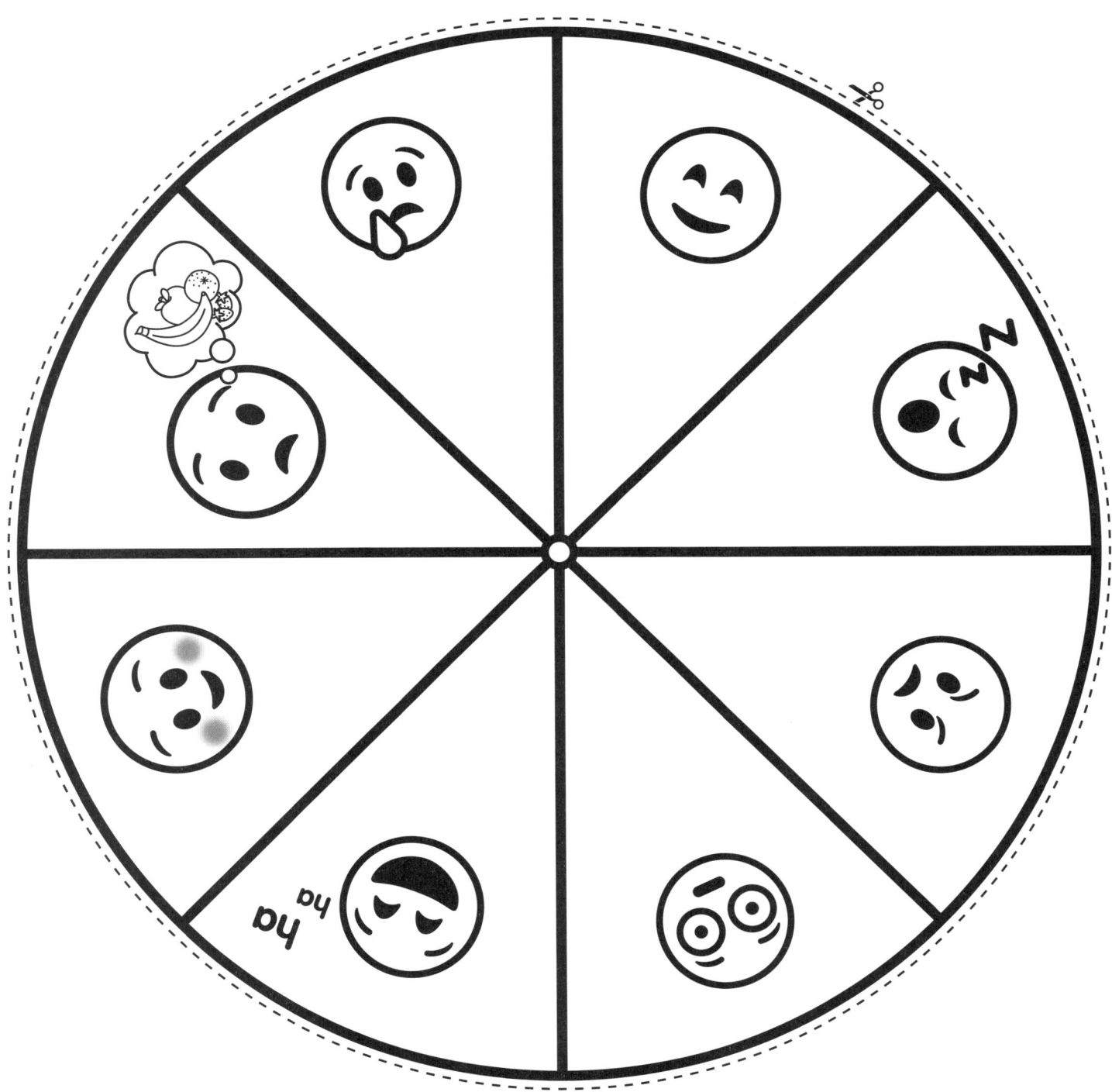

LET YOUR FEELINGS SHOW

Game Sheet

Name _____

Spin the paper clip on the wheel.
Look at the picture that the paper clip lands on.
Then write a spelling word from the box that tells about the picture.

| laugh | smile | tired | angry | shy | scared | sob | hungry |

Spin 1:

Spin 2:

Spin 3:

Spin 4:

CLEAN MOUTH

Practice spelling and using these words about teeth.

- ☐ tooth
- ☐ fairy
- ☐ brush
- ☐ cavity

- ☐ loose
- ☐ floss
- ☐ mouth
- ☐ rinse

SPELLING TIPS

☆ Some words end with the **consonant digraphs sh** and **th**. Digraphs are two letters that have one sound.

☆ The letter pairs **br** and **fl** are **consonant blends**. Consonant blends have two sounds that are said together.

☆ Some words that end with **y** can have a **long e** sound.

CLEAN MOUTH

Tooth Fairy

Name _____

Make a path for the Tooth Fairy to get to the tooth.
Color the words that end in **sh** or **th**.

START	fairy	brush	mouth	tooth
tooth	loose	tooth	rinse	brush
brush	floss	mouth	loose	mouth
mouth	tooth	brush	cavity	tooth
cavity	rinse	fairy	floss	brush
fairy	floss	rinse	loose	END

22 CLEAN MOUTH · Spelling Games and Activities • EMC 8271 • © Evan-Moor Corporation

CLEAN MOUTH

Name _____

My Two Front Teeth

Cut out the letters.
Glue them on the teeth to spell a word from the box.

| fairy   tooth   mouth |

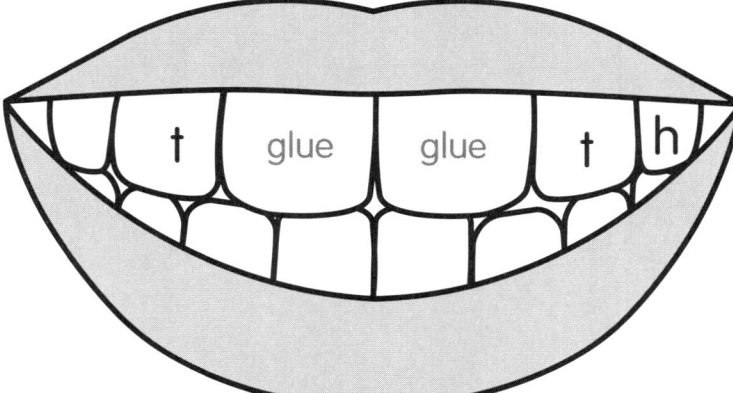

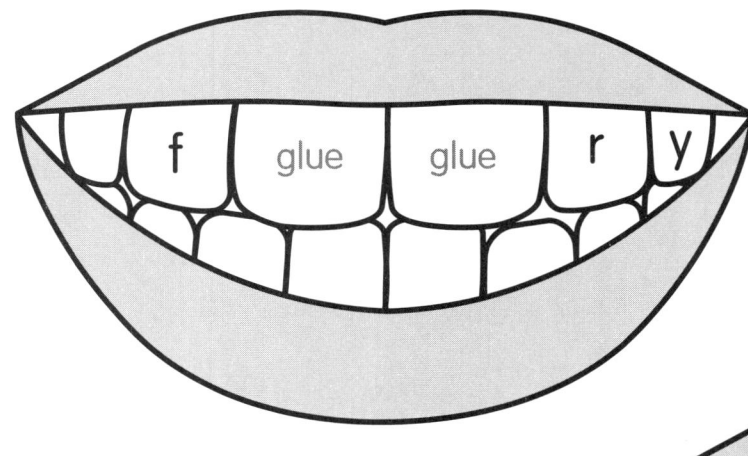

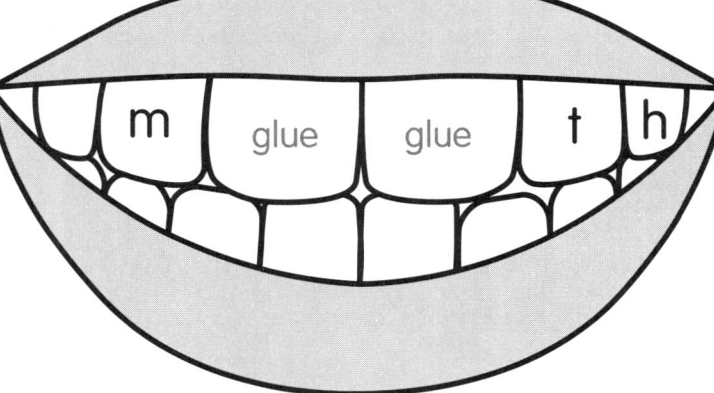

CLEAN MOUTH 23

CLEAN MOUTH

Time to Brush

Name _____

Read the clock.
Match the time to a word with a short vowel sound.
Then write the word to tell what the child needs to do.

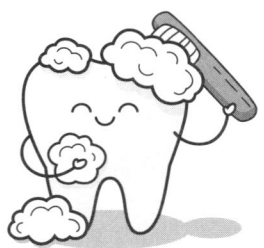

| 10:00 | 3:00 | 7:00 |
| brush | rinse | floss |

CLEAN MOUTH

Brush Your Teeth

Name _____

Help give the children what they need to brush their teeth.
Look at the clue under each child.
Cut out the toothbrushes and tubes of toothpaste on page 26.
Glue them to match. You will not use all of the cutouts.

My toothbrush and toothpaste have words that end with a **long e** sound.

My toothbrush and toothpaste have words that begin with the **blends fl** and **br**.

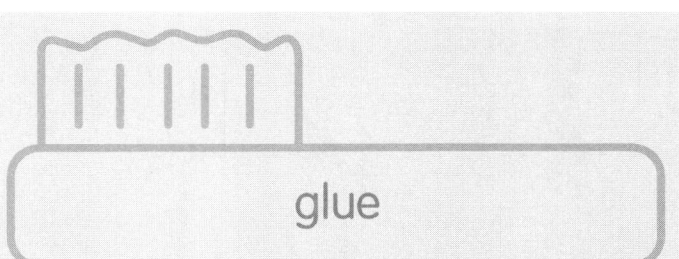

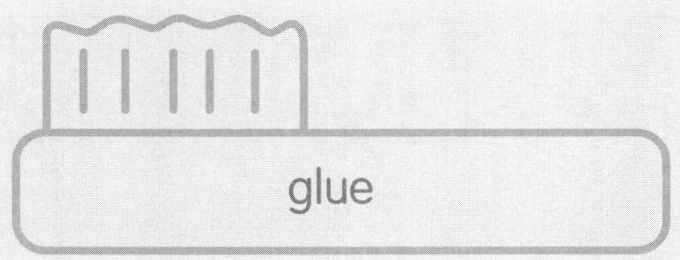

CLEAN MOUTH

Brush Your Teeth, *continued*

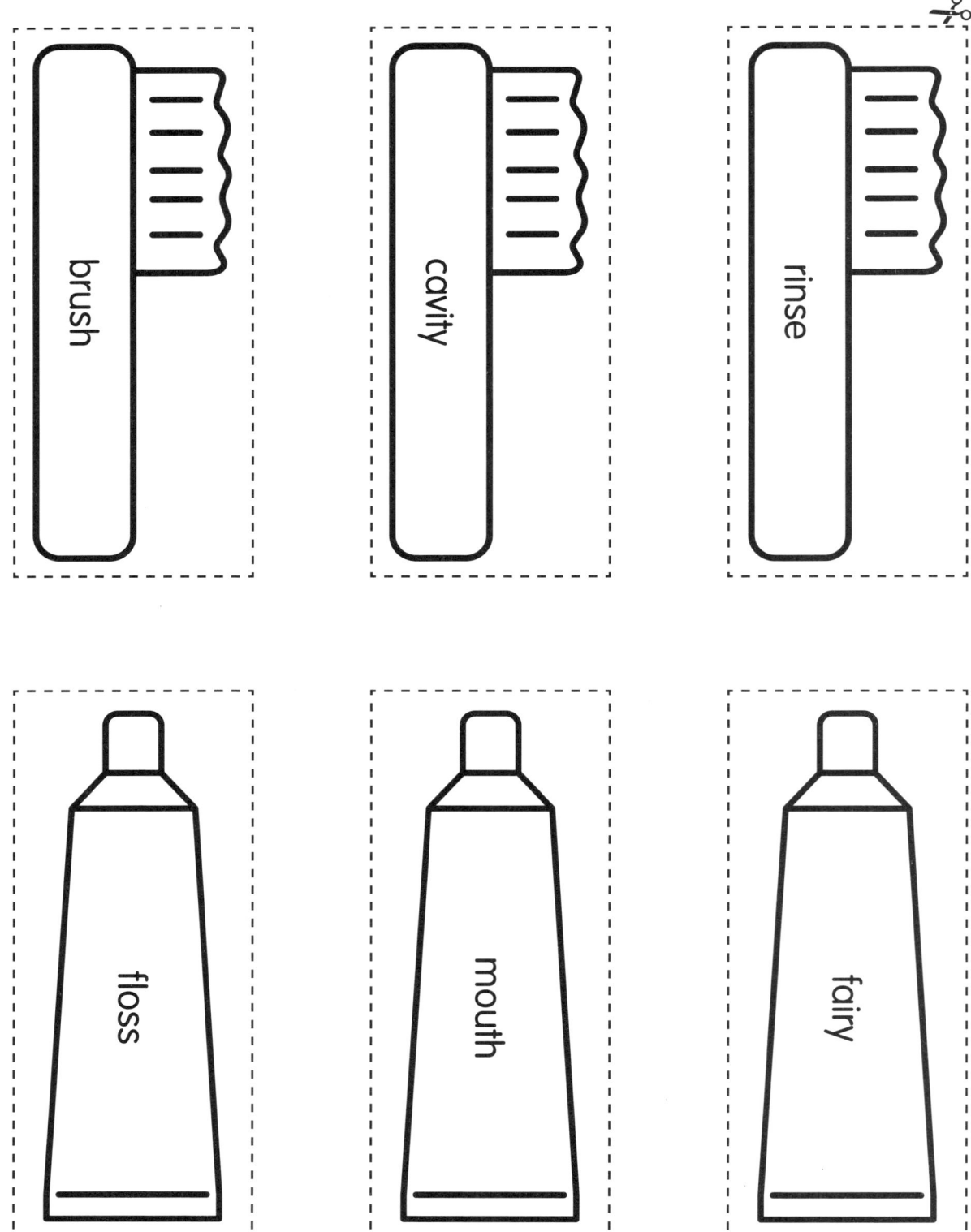

26 CLEAN MOUTH

CLEAN MOUTH

Toothache

Oh no! Each child has a toothache. Unscramble the letters to spell a word from the box to help make the child feel better.

| floss   cavity   loose   mouth |

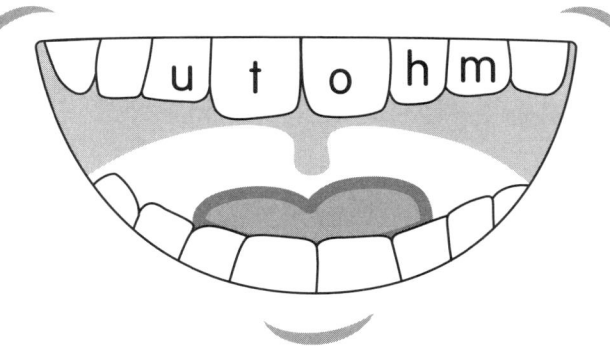
u t o h m

_ _ _ _ _

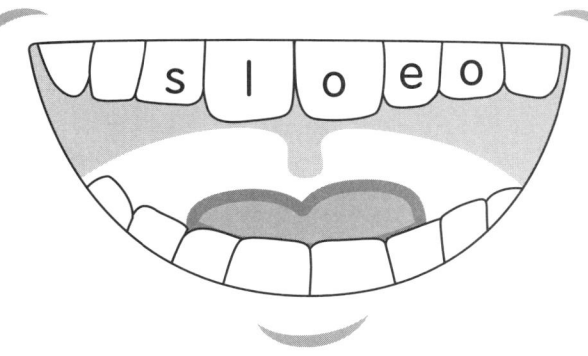
s l o e o

_ _ _ _ _

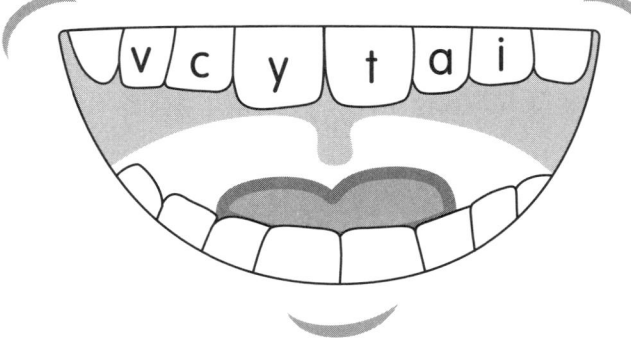
v c y t a i

_ _ _ _ _ _

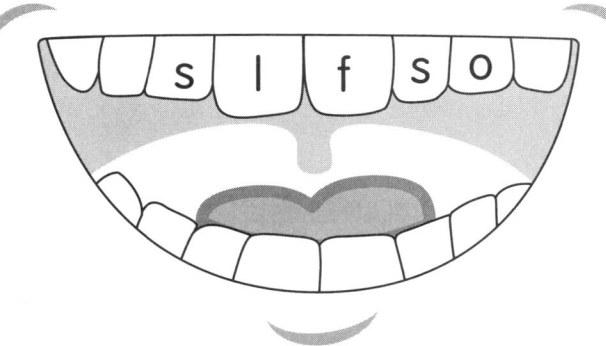
s l f s o

_ _ _ _ _

CLEAN MOUTH

Big Mouth

Students have fun spelling words by pulling teeth through a big mouth.

What You Need

- Big Mouth Slider on page 29
- Letter Pull Tabs on page 30
- scissors

What You Do

1. Print a copy of the Big Mouth Slider and Letter Pull Tabs for each student and one for teacher demonstration.
2. Make one slider for each student and an example to demonstrate with:
   - Cut out the Big Mouth Slider and Letter Pull Tabs.
   - Make cuts along the dotted lines on the Big Mouth Slider.
   - Weave the tab labeled 1 through the first slot on the left. Repeat, pulling tabs 2 and 3 through the other two slots.
3. Explain to students that you will call out a spelling word. Demonstrate how students will spell the word by pulling the tabs through the mouth.
4. Distribute a completed Big Mouth Slider with the Letter Pull Tabs to each student.
5. As students finish spelling each word, have them smile big to let you know that they are ready for the next word.

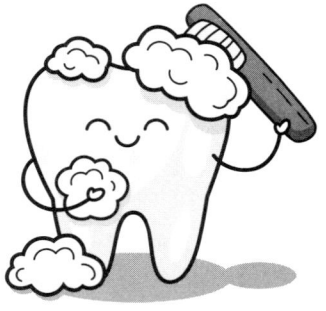

CLEAN MOUTH

Big Mouth Slider

Clean Mouth
Letter Pull Tabs

1	2	3
t	u	ss
br	oo	th
fl	ai	sh
ca	in	ty
f	o	ry
l	ou	se
r	vi	
m		

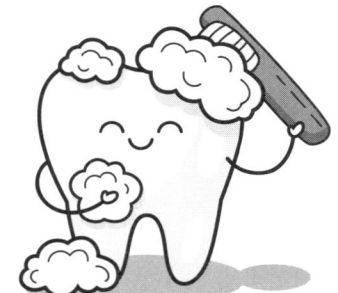

IN THE KITCHEN

Practice spelling and using these words about food.

- ☐ ice
- ☐ cook
- ☐ food
- ☐ juice
- ☐ fruit
- ☐ slice
- ☐ mix
- ☐ scoop

SPELLING TIPS

★ The letter **c** can have a **soft** sound like you hear in **ice** or a **hard** sound like you hear in **cat**.

★ Vowel pairs have one sound.
  - The vowel pair **ui** can have a **long u** sound.
  - The vowel pair **oo** can have the sound you hear in **food**. It can also have the sound you hear in **cook**.

★ The letter pairs **fr**, **sc**, and **sl** are **consonant blends**. Consonant blends have two sounds that are said together.

Cups of Ice

IN THE KITCHEN

Read the spelling rule below each cup.
Then write the missing letter or letters on each ice cube.

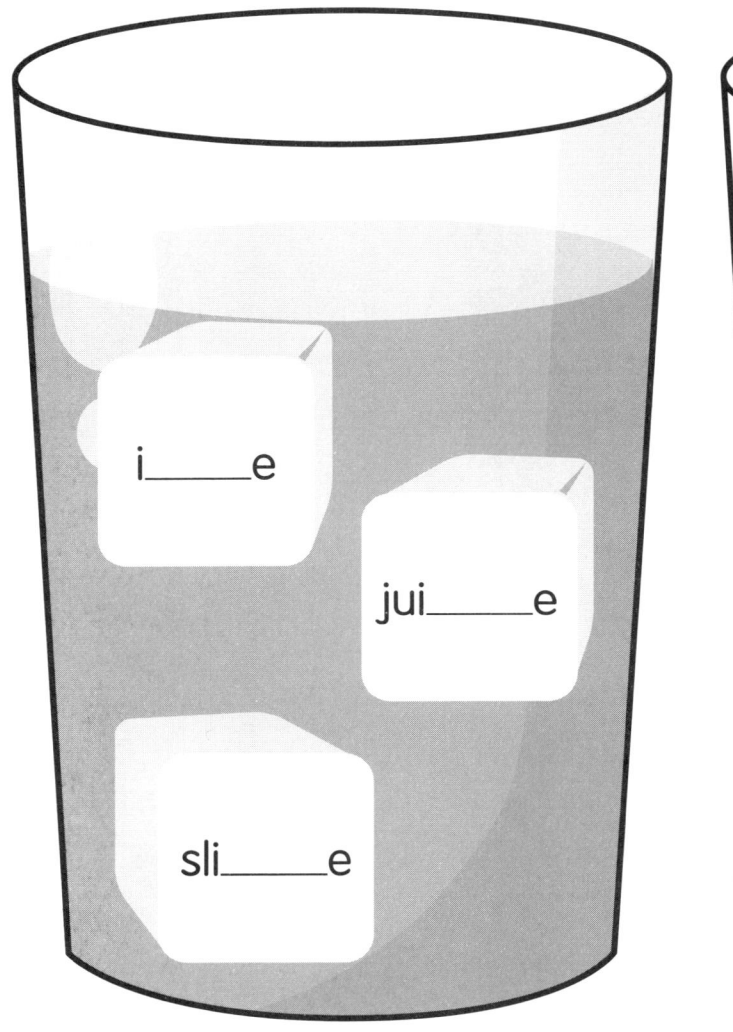

has soft c

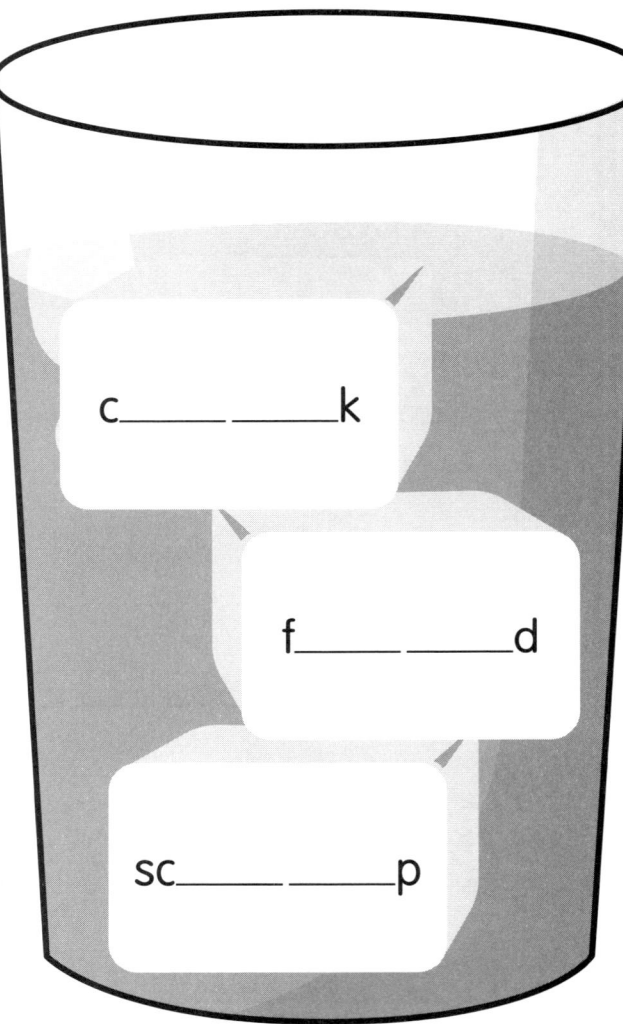

has letter pair oo

IN THE KITCHEN

Spelling Recipe

Read the clue below the line.
Then write a word from the box to complete the recipe.

| ice | fruit | cook | food |
| slice | mix | juice | scoop |

Put a _____ of bread in a pan.
(begins with **s**)

Put the _____ into a bowl.
(begins with **fr**)

Use a spoon and _____ it all together.
(ends with **x**)

_____ the mix into a pan.
(begins with **sc**)

Then _____ it in the oven.
(begins with **c**)

Eat your _____ with a glass of
(has **oo**)
_____ with _____. Enjoy!
(has **soft c**)   (has **soft c**)

Set the Table

It is time for dinner!
Read the clue in each box on the table. Write a spelling word.
Then draw the picture that matches the word to set the table.

ice   cook   juice   food   fruit

begins with a **hard c**	has a **long u** sound
_____	_____

has a **long i** sound

_____

begins with **fr**	has the vowel pair **oo**
_____	_____

Name ______________________________

Piece of Cake

Cut out the cake pieces on page 36. Then read the clue on the cake stand. Glue the letters on the cake to spell the correct word from the box.

ice	fruit	cook	mix

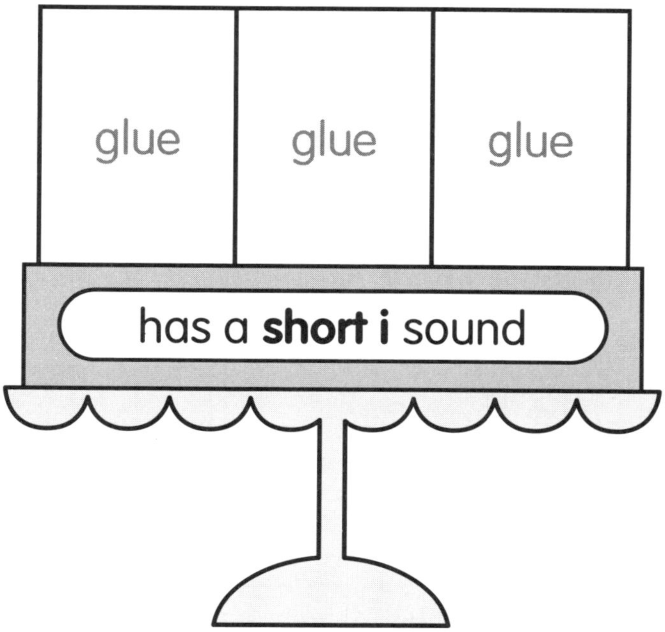
glue
glue
glue
has a **short i** sound

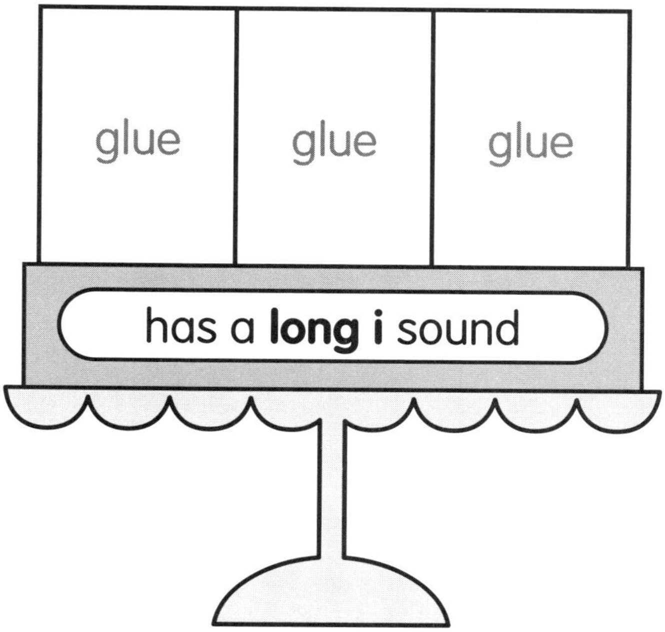
glue
glue
glue
has a **long i** sound

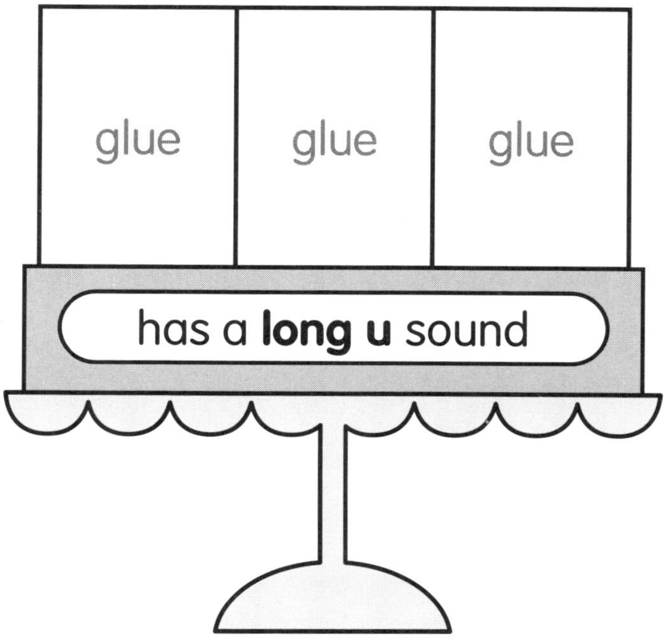
glue
glue
glue
has a **long u** sound

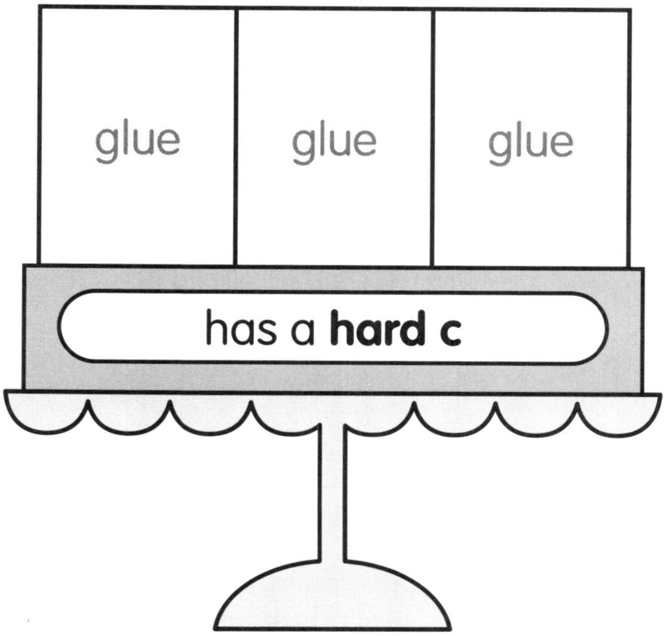
glue
glue
glue
has a **hard c**

IN THE KITCHEN

Piece of Cake

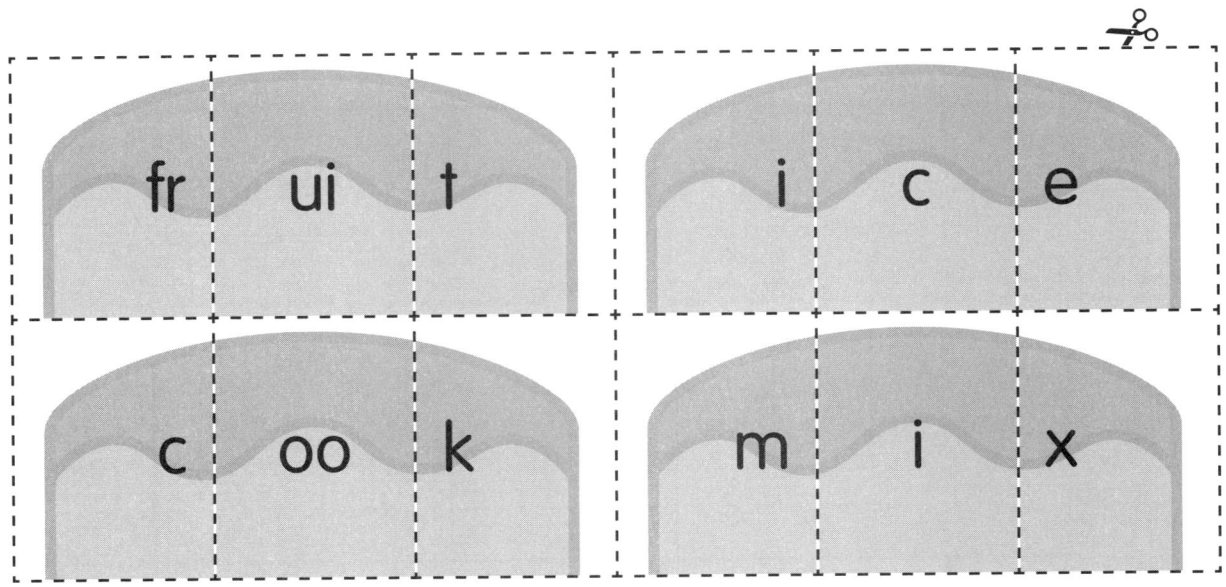

36 IN THE KITCHEN

IN THE KITCHEN

Lunch Order Mix-up

Name _____

Oh no! The chef mixed up the letters in each food order! Unscramble the letters to spell a word. Then draw a line to match the words and give each child his or her lunch.

 r u f i t

_____ •

 • food

 c i u j e

_____ •

 • fruit

 f d o o

_____ •

 • slice

 e s c i l

_____ •

 • juice

(IN THE KITCHEN)

Name _____

Hot Potato

Students have fun spelling words that match clues by playing Hot Potato. But they must write quickly, because the words are hot potatoes!

What You Need

- Hot Potato Die on page 39
- Hot Potato Words on page 40
- scissors
- glue
- pencil

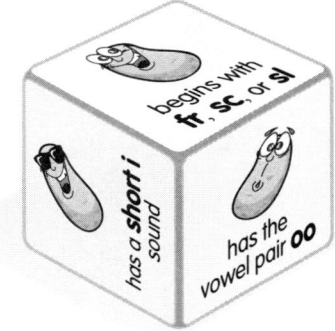

How to Play

1. Print a copy of the Hot Potato Die for each group of four students. Print a copy of the Hot Potato Words for each student.

2. Cut out each Hot Potato Die and assemble it by folding and gluing the tabs.

3. Put students into groups of four.

4. Distribute a pencil and a Hot Potato Words sheet to each student and one die for each group of students.

5. Explain to students that they will take turns rolling the die and writing a word.

6. On each turn, a player rolls the die and reads the clue that is facing up. The player finds a spelling word that matches the clue and picks up the die. The player writes the word on the Hot Potato Words sheet quickly, because the potato on the die is hot! Once the player spells the word, he or she tosses the Hot Potato Die to another person in the group.

7. Repeat until every player rolls at least three or more times, or for as long as time allows.

IN THE KITCHEN
Hot Potato Die

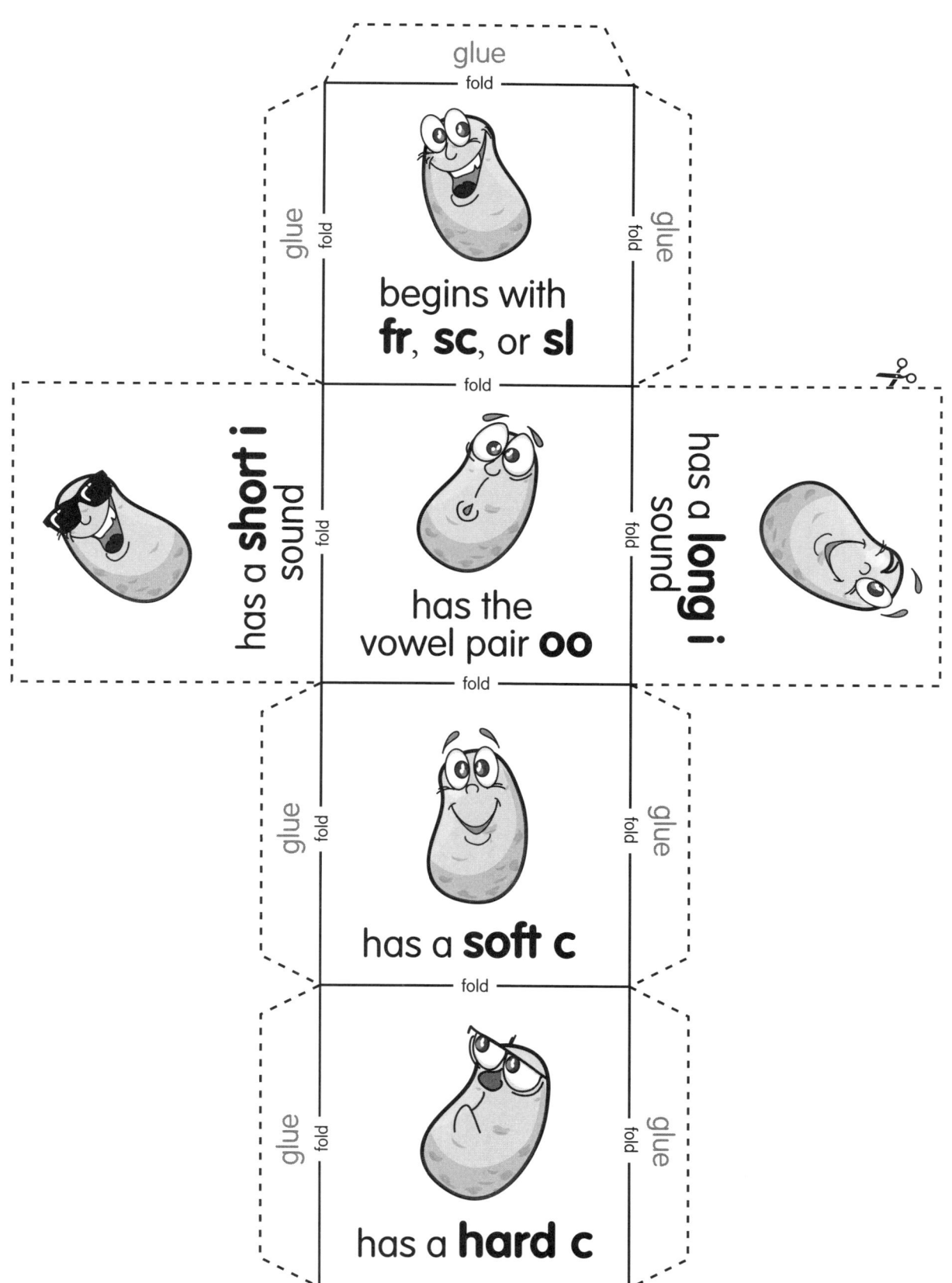

In the Kitchen

Hot Potato Words

Name _____

 1. Roll the Hot Potato Die.

 2. Read the clue on the die.

 3. Then write a spelling word from the box that matches the clue.

| cook | food | fruit | ice |
| juice | mix | scoop | slice |

Roll 1:

Roll 2:

Roll 3:

IN THE GARDEN

Practice spelling and using these words about things in a garden.

- ☐ butterfly
- ☐ spider
- ☐ dragonfly
- ☐ beetle
- ☐ grasshopper
- ☐ dirt
- ☐ ladybug
- ☐ flower

SPELLING TIPS

☆ The words **dirt** and **spider** have **r-controlled** vowels. The **r** changes the sound of the vowel.

☆ The words **butterfly** and **ladybug** are **compound** words. Compound words are two words that are put together to make one word.

☆ The letter pairs **dr**, **fl**, **gr**, and **sp** are **consonant blends**. Consonant blends have two sounds that are said together.

Garden Drawings

Draw the other half.
Then write a word from the box that tells about the picture.

butterfly   flower   ladybug   spider

_____

_____

_____

_____

Flower Garden

Color the flower 🖍 RED if the word has **ee**.
Color the flower 🖍 YELLOW if the word has an **r** after a vowel.
Color the flower 🖍 PINK if the word is a **compound** word.

Life in the Garden

Write a word from the box to tell about the picture.

> beetle   butterfly   dirt   dragonfly
> flower   grasshopper   spider

IN THE GARDEN | Name _____

Through the Garden

Help the bugs get through the garden by following a spelling word. Color the squares to spell a word. Look at the example.

grasshopper

START →

g	r	a	s
n	l	q	s
c	p	o	h
v	p	d	b
r	e	u	s

END

butterfly

← START

a	d	u	b
e	t	t	s
r	p	o	h
f	l	d	b
r	y	u	s

END

ladybug

START →

l	i	a	s
a	d	j	h
i	y	b	h
z	p	u	q
y	w	g	d

END

spider

← START

g	y	p	s
q	b	i	b
a	j	d	u
m	z	e	f
r	o	r	t

END

© Evan-Moor Corporation • EMC 8271 • Spelling Games and Activities

IN THE GARDEN
Web of Flies

Name _____

What did the spider catch in its web?
Cut and glue the pictures from page 47. Then write the missing letters to tell which bug was caught in the web.

____ ____agonfly

lady____ ____ ____

b____ ____tle

butter____ ____y

> IN THE GARDEN

Web of Flies Cutouts

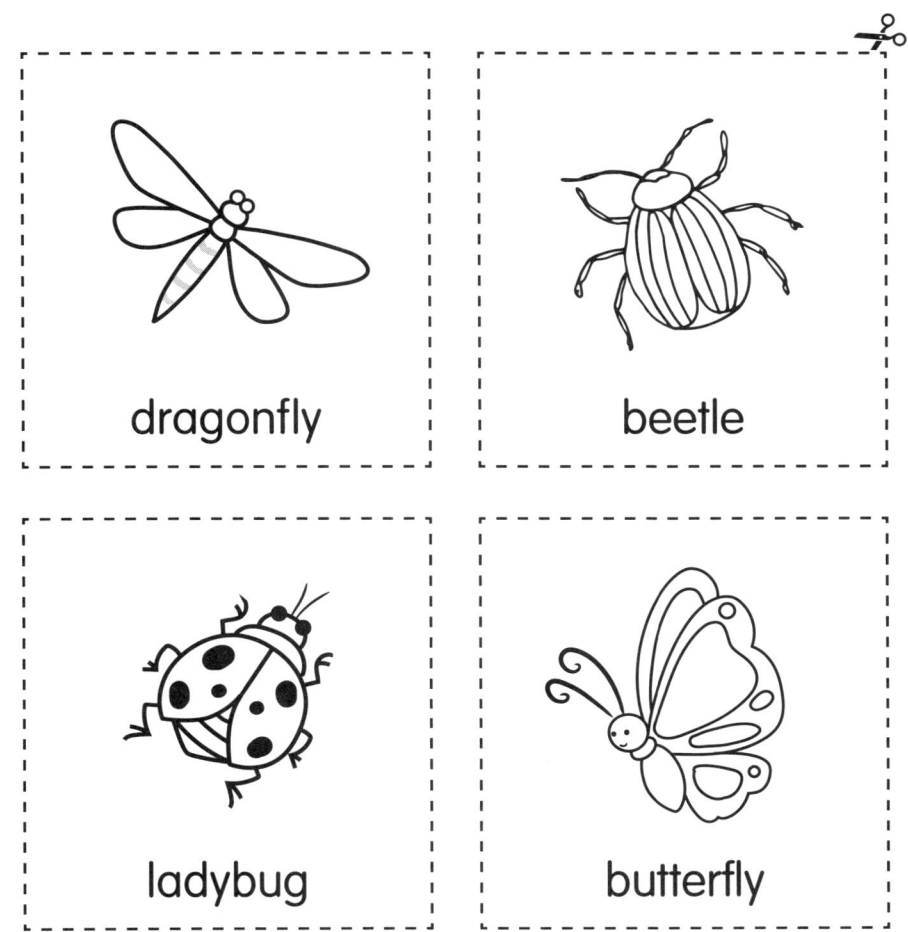

IN THE GARDEN 47

IN THE GARDEN

Name _____

Memory Garden

Students have fun spelling words by matching cards and spelling what they see!

What You Need

- In the Garden spelling word list on page 41
- Garden Cards on pages 49 and 50
- scissors
- lined paper
- pencil

How to Play

1. Print a copy of the spelling word list and the Garden Cards for each pair of students. Cut out the cards.

2. Put students into pairs. Distribute a set of cards and the spelling word list to each pair. Distribute a sheet of paper and a pencil to each student.

3. Model how to place all the cards facedown in four rows of four cards (see example).

4. Explain to students that they will be looking for matching cards. The first player flips over two cards.

   - If the cards have **different** pictures, the player's turn is over, and the next player has a turn.
   - If the cards have the **same** picture, the partner reads the matching word from the spelling list. The player writes the word that tells about the card. If the spelling is correct, the player keeps the cards. Then it is the other player's turn.

   Repeat until all matching pairs are found.

5. Have players count their matching pairs. The player with the most pairs of cards wins.

Card setup

IN THE GARDEN

Garden Cards

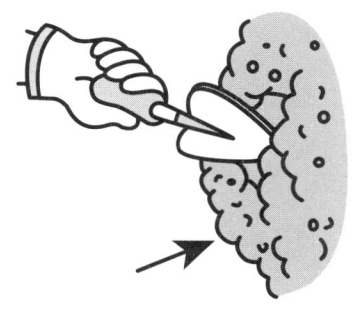 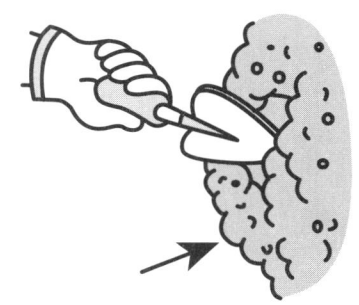

IN THE GARDEN
Garden Cards, continued

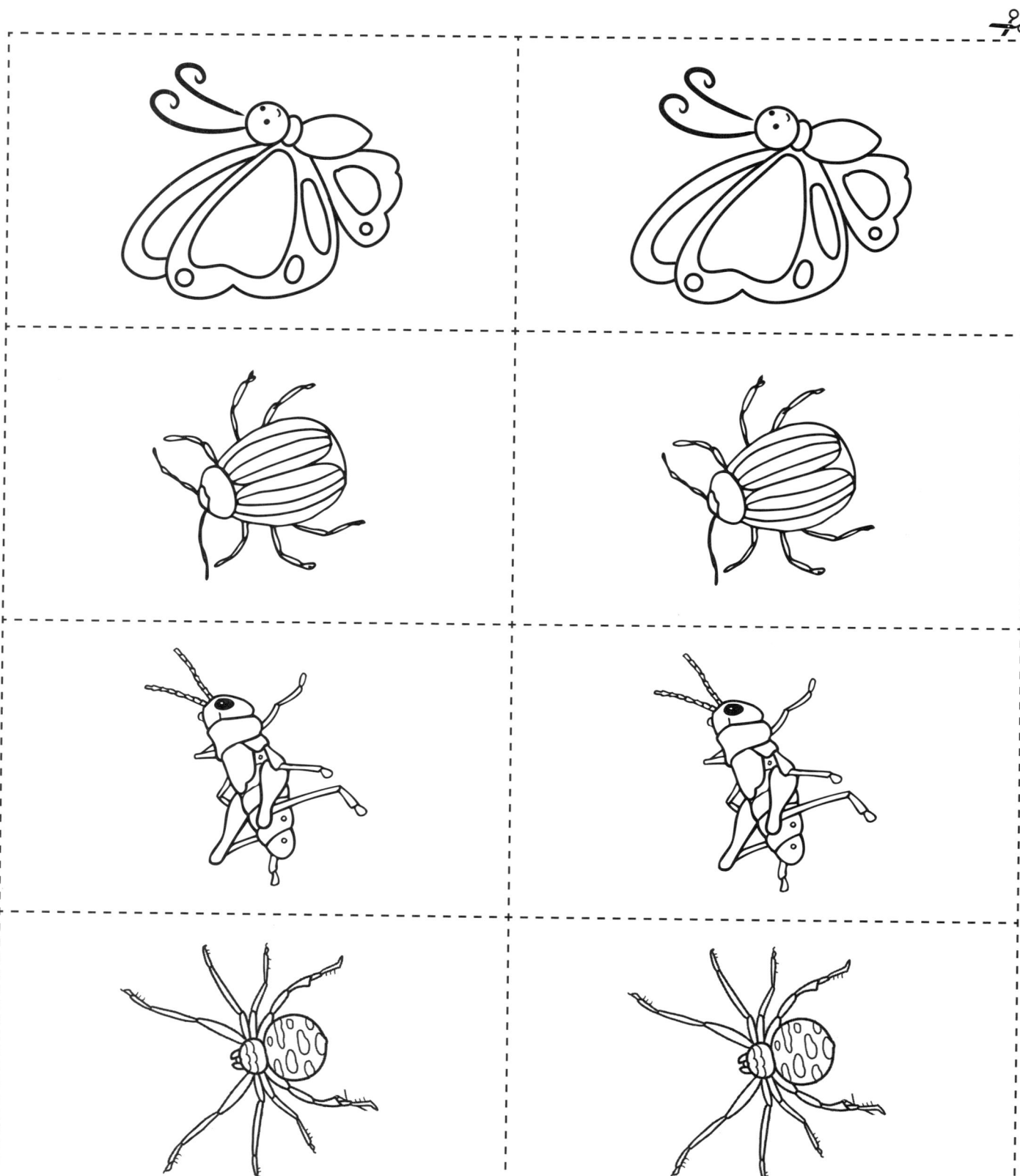

FUN AT THE FAIR

Name _____

Practice spelling and using these words about the fair.

- ☐ fair
- ☐ wheel
- ☐ fried
- ☐ booth
- ☐ scream
- ☐ spin
- ☐ prize
- ☐ ribbon

SPELLING TIPS

☆ The letter groups **fr**, **pr**, **sp**, and **scr** are **consonant blends**. Consonant blends have two or more sounds that are said together.

☆ The vowel pairs **ai**, **ea**, **ee**, **ie**, and **oo** have one sound.

FUN AT THE FAIR
Ride Tickets

Name _____

Read the sign about riding on Scream Machine. Help the girl write the missing letters on each ticket to see if she can go on the ride. Then answer the questions.

Scream Machine

You need **3 tickets** that begin with **sp**, **pr**, or **scr** to go on this ride.

spin   booth   prize   scream

_____ eam

_____ in

_____ ize

boo _____

How many tickets have a word that starts with these letters? _____

Can the girl ride on Scream Machine? Circle.

 yes

 no

52 FUN AT THE FAIR   Spelling Games and Activities • EMC 8271 • © Evan-Moor Corporation

Twice the Letters, Twice the Fun!

Some people on the Ferris wheel want to go around again.
Circle the pods on the Ferris wheel that have a word with a **double letter**.

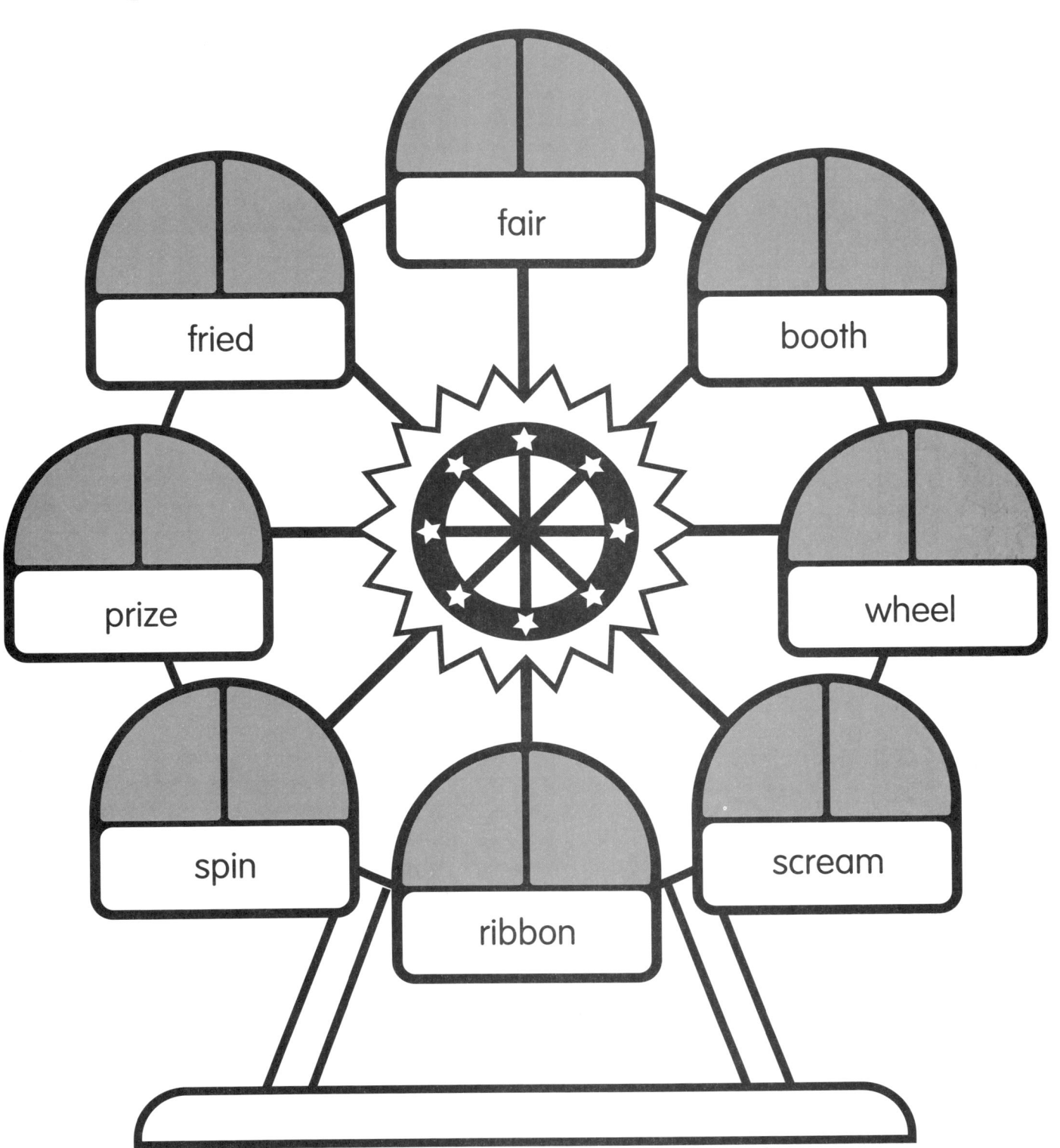

Bumper Cars

FUN AT THE FAIR

Name _____

Bump cars to spell a word. Look at the word. Draw a line to each letter to spell the word. The first line has been drawn.

wheel

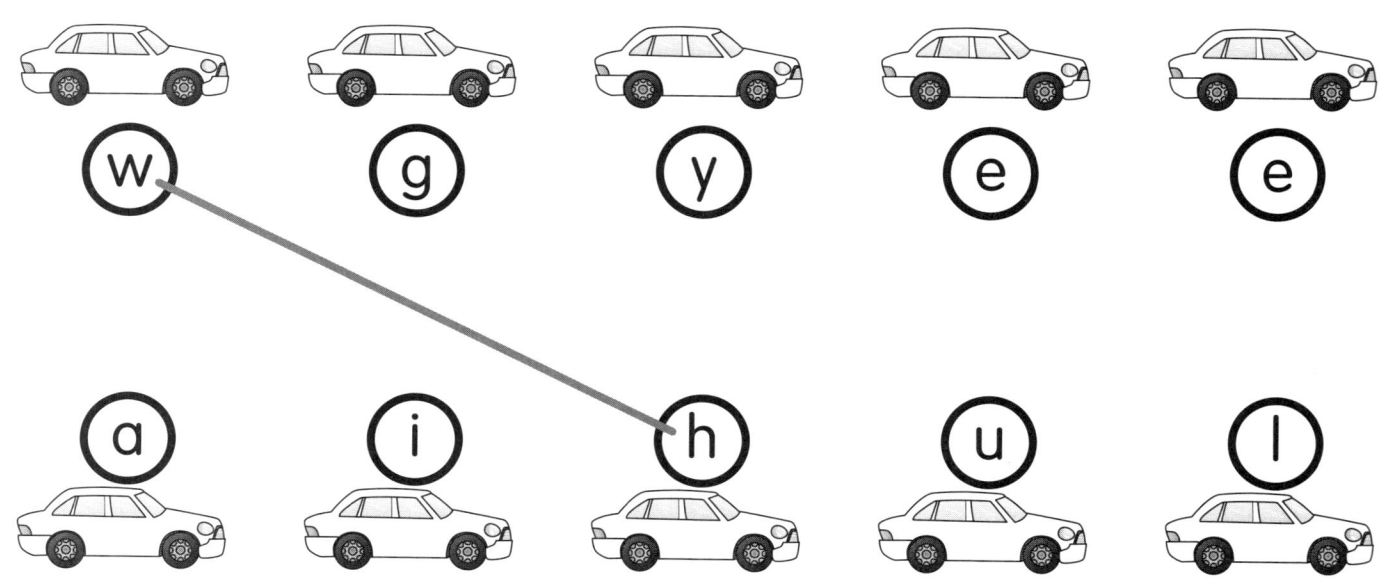

ribbon

FUN AT THE FAIR

Knock Them Down

Look at the word on each can. Knock down the cans that have a long vowel sound by marking them with an **X**.

(FUN AT THE FAIR)   Name _____

You're a Winner!

All the children won a prize at the fair.

Unscramble the letters to spell a word from the box. Then draw a line to match the words and give each child his or her prize.

| fair | spin | ribbon | booth |

brobin   afri   thobo   pins

spin   fair   ribbon   booth

(FUN AT THE FAIR)

Fair Map

Write a word from the box to label each place on the map.

Welcome to the _____

Fried   Scream
Prize   Wheel
Fair   Spin

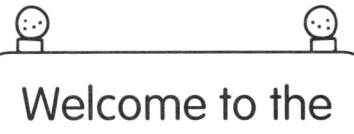

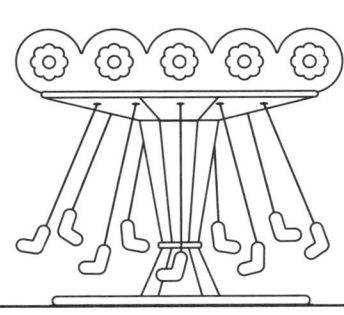

_____ Around

Ferris _____

_____ Shop

Ride the Big Scream!

_____ Foods

Big _____ Coaster

FUN AT THE FAIR

Name _____

Roller Coaster Game

Students have fun spelling words as they take a ride along a roller coaster game board.

What You Need

- Fun at the Fair spelling word list on page 51
- Die and Coaster Cars on page 59
- Game Board on page 60
- scissors
- glue

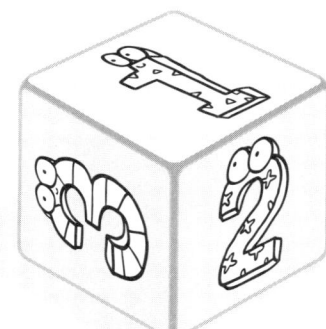

How to Play

1. Print a copy of the Die and Coaster Cars and the Game Board for every pair of students.
2. Cut out the pieces and make the dice for the students.
   - Cut out the coaster cars. Fold the bottoms to make them stand.
   - Cut out each die and assemble it by folding and gluing the tabs.
3. Put students into pairs.
4. Distribute one die, two coaster cars, two spelling word lists, and one game board to each pair of students. Have them place their coaster cars on the START space.
5. Explain to students that they will take turns rolling the die and moving along the game board.
6. On each turn, a player rolls the die and moves his or her coaster car the same number of squares. The player then spells a word from the spelling word list that follows the spelling pattern on the square he or she lands on.
7. Repeat until a player reaches the END space and wins.

FUN AT THE FAIR
Die and Coaster Cars

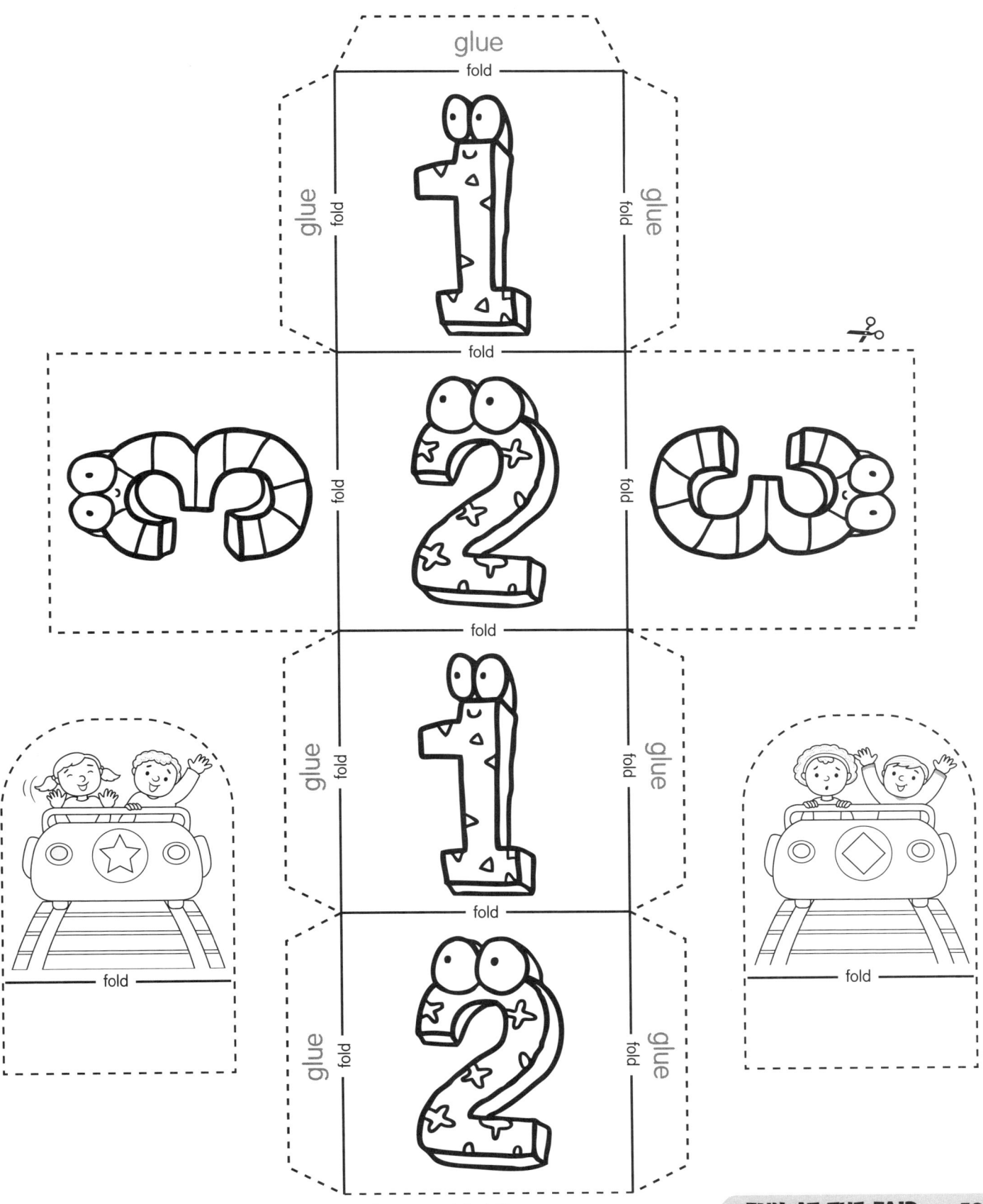

© Evan-Moor Corporation • EMC 8271 • Spelling Games and Activities

FUN AT THE FAIR
Game Board

START
- Long vowel sound
- Begins with fr, pr, sp, or scr
- Has a double letter
- Short vowel sound
- Has a vowel pair
- Long vowel sound
- Has a double letter
- Short vowel sound
- Begins with fr, pr, sp, or scr
- Has a vowel pair
- Long vowel sound
- Begins with fr, pr, sp, or scr

END

RAINY DAYS

Practice spelling and using these words about rainy days.

- ☐ cloud
- ☐ rainbow
- ☐ boots
- ☐ jacket
- ☐ storm
- ☐ splash
- ☐ puddle
- ☐ umbrella

SPELLING TIPS

☆ The vowel pair **ou** in **cloud** is a **diphthong**. Diphthongs have two vowel sounds that are said together.

☆ The letter groups **br**, **cl**, **spl**, and **st** are **consonant blends**. Consonant blends have two or more sounds that are said together.

☆ The letter pair **sh** in **splash** is a **consonant digraph**. Digraphs are two letters that have one sound.

Colors of the Rainbow

RAINY DAYS

Color the rainbow.

Use GREEN if the word has **dd**.
Use YELLOW if the word has **ai**.
Use RED if the word has **sh**.
Use PURPLE if the word has **ou**.
Use BLUE if the word has **oo**.

splash

rainbow

puddle

boots

cloud

RAINY DAYS

Under the Umbrella

Read the spelling rule. Then write the missing letters to make a word from the box.

| boots | cloud | puddle |
| splash | storm | umbrella |

____ ____oud

____ ____ ____ash

____ ____orm

b____ ____ts

pu____ ____le

umbre____ ____a

RAINY DAYS

Name _____

Splashing in Puddles

Make a path for the duckling to get home.
Color the words that start with **cl**, **spl**, or **st**.

START →

| cloud | splash | storm |

| boots | puddle | jacket | cloud |

| splash | cloud | storm | splash |

| storm | jacket | rainbow | umbrella |

| cloud | splash | storm |

HOME

64 RAINY DAYS · Spelling Games and Activities • EMC 8271 • © Evan-Moor Corporation

RAINY DAYS

Raining Letters

It's raining letters!
Cut out the raindrops at the bottom of the page.
Glue them to spell a word.

umbrella   jacket   boots   rainbow

 b glue glue t s

 j a glue glue e t

 r glue glue n b o w

 u m b glue e l glue a

l k o i c o r a

RAINY DAYS

Rainy Day Dress-up

Name _____

Cooper has everything he needs to play in the rain. Others want to play, too. But each child is missing something he or she needs to keep dry.

Look at the pictures. Write what each child needs.

umbrella   jacket   boots

Cooper

_____   _____   _____

66 RAINY DAYS   Spelling Games and Activities • EMC 8271 • © Evan-Moor Corporation

Rainy Day Rhymes

Write a word or words from the box to finish the rhyme.

| rainbow   splash   storm   umbrella   puddle |

Under the _____ we like to cuddle, as we watch

the ducks _____ in the _____.

After the _____, we see a great show,

all the pretty colors of the _____.

RAINY DAYS

Rainy Day Puzzle

Students have fun using their spelling words to help them complete a puzzle.

What You Need

- Puzzle Pieces on pages 69 and 70
- scissors

What You Do

1. Print a copy of the puzzle pieces for each student.
2. Distribute the puzzle pieces and a pair of scissors to each student.
3. Have students cut out the pieces along the dotted lines.
4. Explain to students that they will use the pieces to make a picture.
5. Students will first match the puzzle pieces together to spell the spelling words. Then they will put all the words together to make a rainy day picture.

RAINY DAYS

Puzzle Pieces

Puzzle Pieces, continued

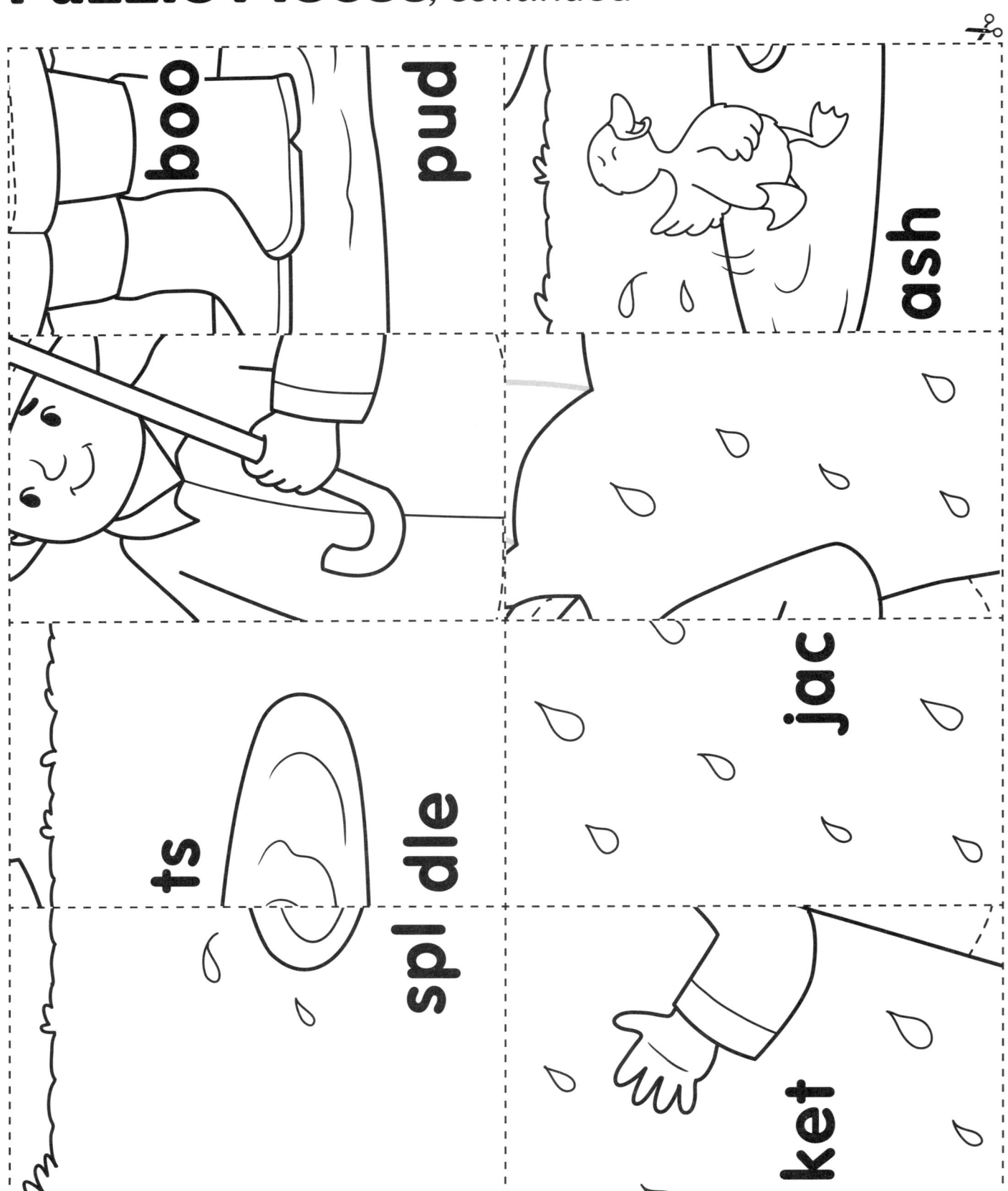

CAMPING IN THE FOREST

Practice spelling and using these words about camping in the forest.

- ☐ forest
- ☐ tent
- ☐ hike
- ☐ cave
- ☐ bear
- ☐ deer
- ☐ mountain
- ☐ backpack

SPELLING TIPS

☆ The words **bear**, **deer**, and **forest** have **r-controlled** vowels. The **r** changes the sound of the vowel.

☆ The word **backpack** is a **compound** word. Compound words are two words that are put together to make one word.

☆ The vowel pair **ou** is a **diphthong**. Diphthongs have two vowel sounds that are said together.

Forest Patterns

Draw what comes next in the pattern.
Then write the word that tells about what you drew.

| bear  | cave  | deer | forest | mountain |

Pattern 1

_____

Pattern 2

_____

Pattern 3

_____

CAMPING IN THE FOREST

Name _____

Sleeping in the Forest

Help the children find their tent. Read the clues.
Then write each child's name under a tent at the campsite.

 Grace's tent has a **long vowel** sound.

 Jackson's tent has a **compound** word.

 Pam's tent has a **short vowel** sound.

 Marvin's tent has a word that is **r-controlled**.

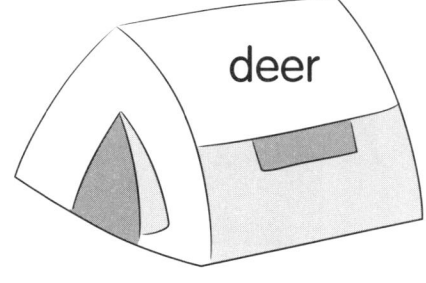

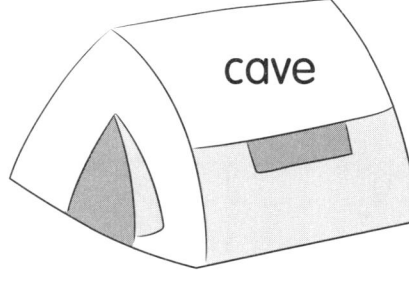

CAMPING IN THE FOREST

Name _____

Spelling by the Campfire

Cut out the letters at the bottom of the page.
Glue them on the marshmallows to spell a word.

| forest | bear | cave |
| deer | mountain | backpack |

d e glue glue

f glue glue e s t

c glue v glue

m glue glue n t a glue n

Which word above has a **silent e**? _____

r a u e o r e o i

74 CAMPING IN THE FOREST

CAMPING IN THE FOREST

Name _____

Through the Forest

Help the hiker get through the forest.
Spell words to tell what she saw on her hike.

bear	backpack
deer	mountain
cave	forest
tent	

CAMPING IN THE FOREST

Name _____

In the Cave

A hiker found a cave, but it was too dark to see what was inside. Cut out the pictures on page 77 and glue them below. Then write the missing letters to tell what is in the cave.

| bear | deer |
| tent | backpack |

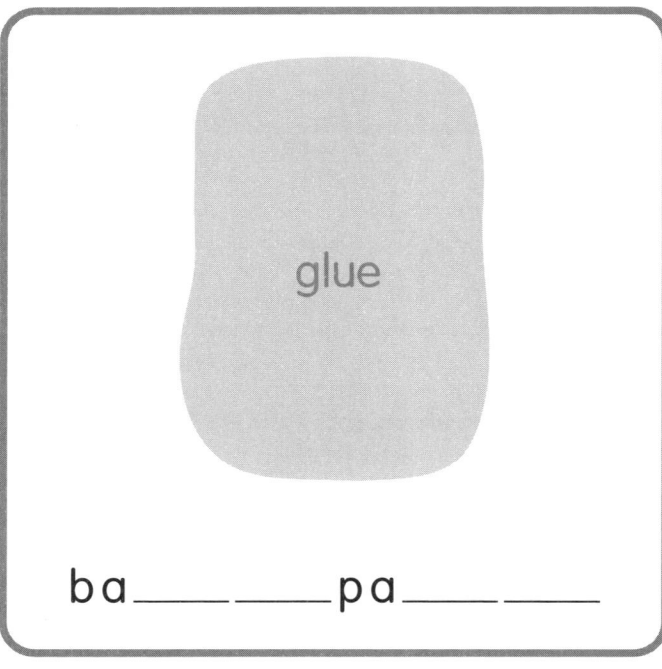

b a ___ ___ p a ___ ___

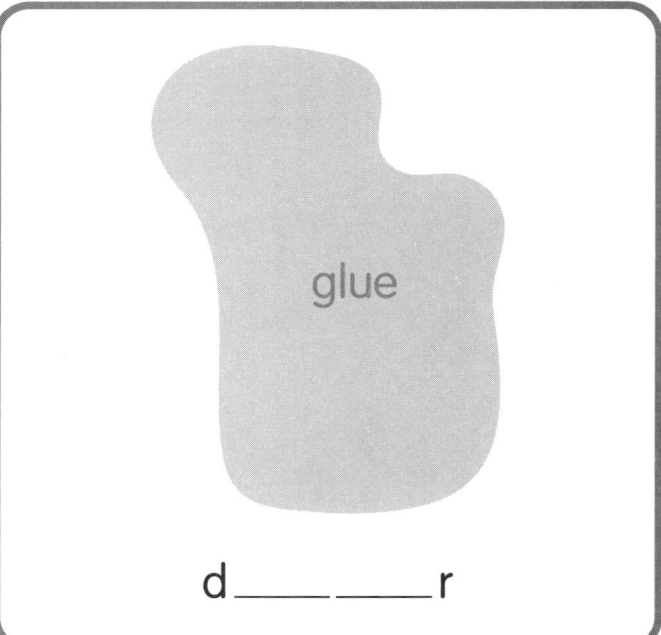

d ___ ___ r

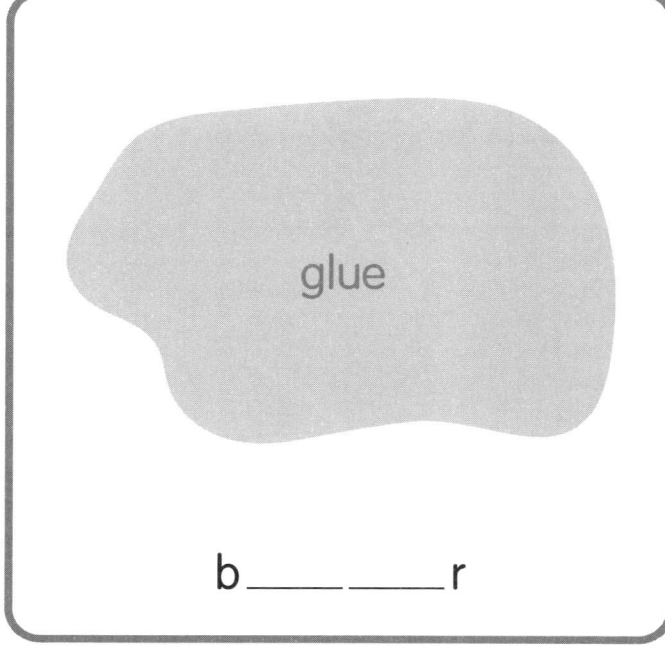

b ___ ___ r

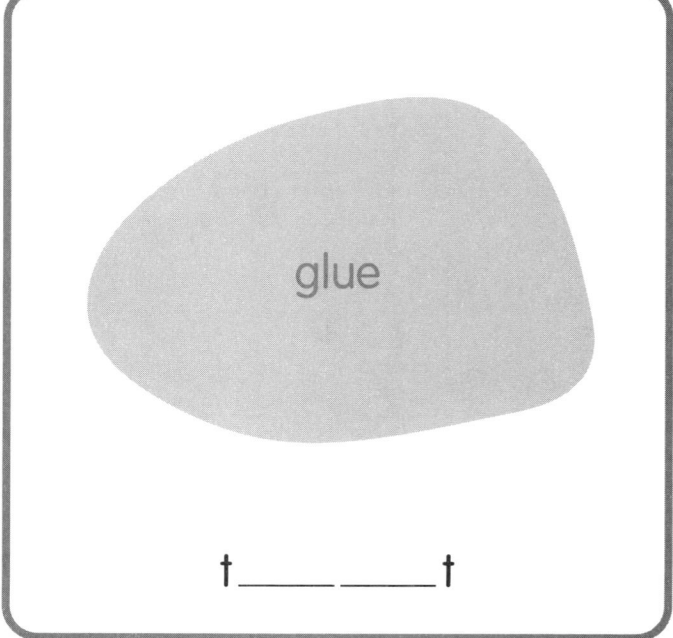

t ___ ___ t

CAMPING IN THE FOREST

Cave Cutouts

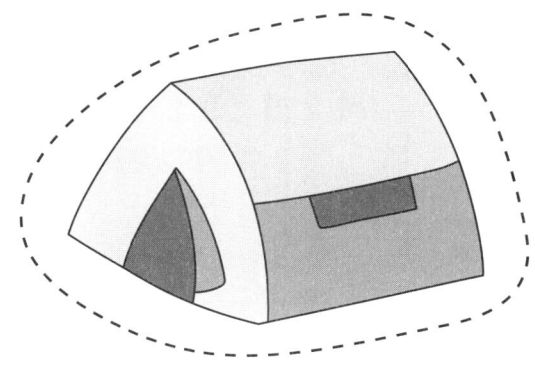

> CAMPING IN THE FOREST

Take a Hike

Students have fun spelling words while playing a card game.

What You Need

- Take a Hike Cards on pages 79 and 80
- card stock, contact paper, or laminator (optional)
- scissors

How to Play

1. Print a copy of the Take a Hike Cards for each pair of students. To make cards more sturdy, copy onto card stock or use contact paper or a laminator to protect paper copies. Then cut out the cards.

2. Put students into pairs and distribute a set of cards to each pair.

3. Model how to shuffle or mix the cards without looking at them and how to deal cards facedown, alternating cards "one for you, one for me." Then have one student in each pair deal 5 cards to both players. The remaining cards are stacked in a pile, facedown.

4. Explain to students that they will play a card game. The goal of the game is to collect the most matching pairs of cards.

5. Player 1 looks at his or her cards and asks Player 2 if he or she has the card needed to make a match and spells the word without looking at the card. For example, "Do you have a mountain? m-o-u-n-t-a-i-n."

    - If Player 2 has that card and Player 1 spelled it correctly, he or she must give it to Player 1.
    - If Player 2 does not have the card or if Player 1 misspelled it, Player 2 says, "Take a Hike." Player 1 chooses the top card from the pile.

    Repeat until all matching pairs are found.

6. Have students count their matching pairs. The player with the most pairs of cards wins!

CAMPING IN THE FOREST
Take a Hike Cards

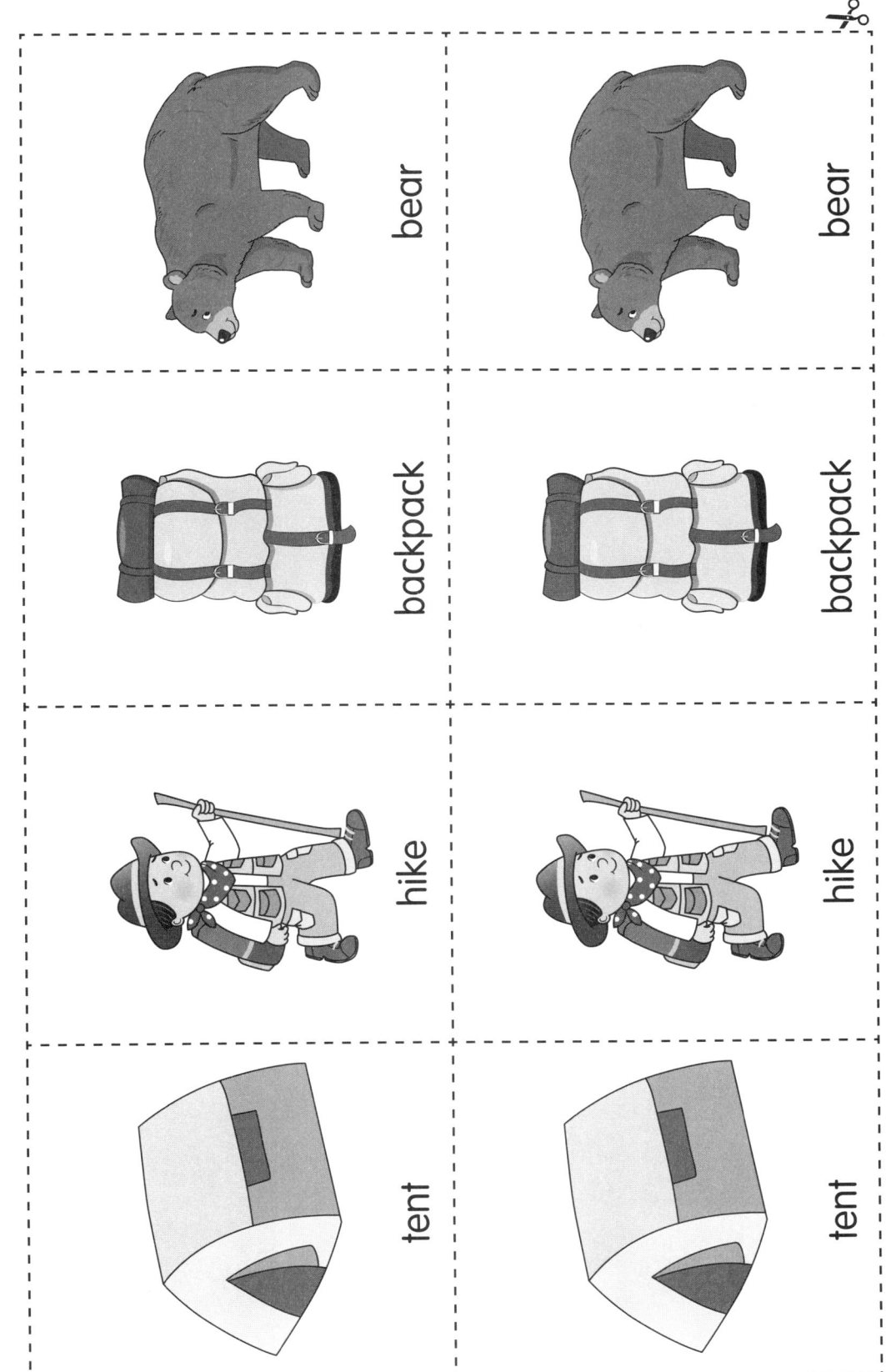

Take a Hike Cards, continued

CAMPING IN THE FOREST

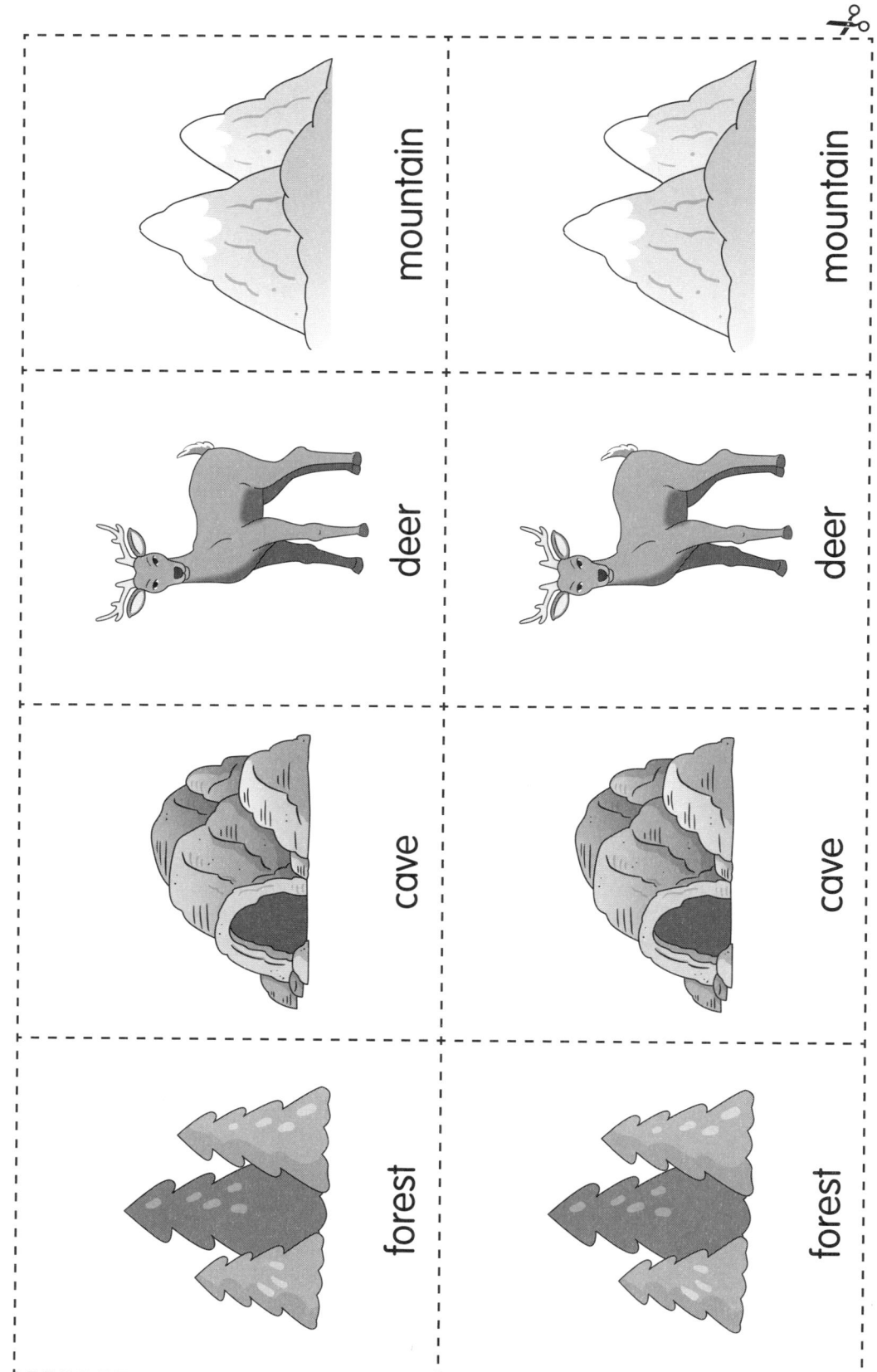

IN THE DEEP BLUE SEA

Practice spelling and using these words about things in the sea.

- ☐ shark
- ☐ crab
- ☐ whale
- ☐ otter

- ☐ jellyfish
- ☐ dolphin
- ☐ seahorse
- ☐ octopus

Spelling Tips

★ The letter pairs **ph**, **sh**, and **wh** are **consonant digraphs**. Digraphs are two letters that have one sound.

★ The letter pair **cr** is a **consonant blend**. Consonant blends have two sounds that are said together.

★ The words **jellyfish** and **seahorse** are **compound** words. Compound words are two words that are put together to make one word.

IN THE DEEP BLUE SEA

Colorful Ocean

Name _____

Color the picture.

Use **YELLOW** for words that begin with a **short o** sound.
Use **PURPLE** for words that have **ph**, **sh**, or **wh**.
Use **BLUE** for **compound** words.

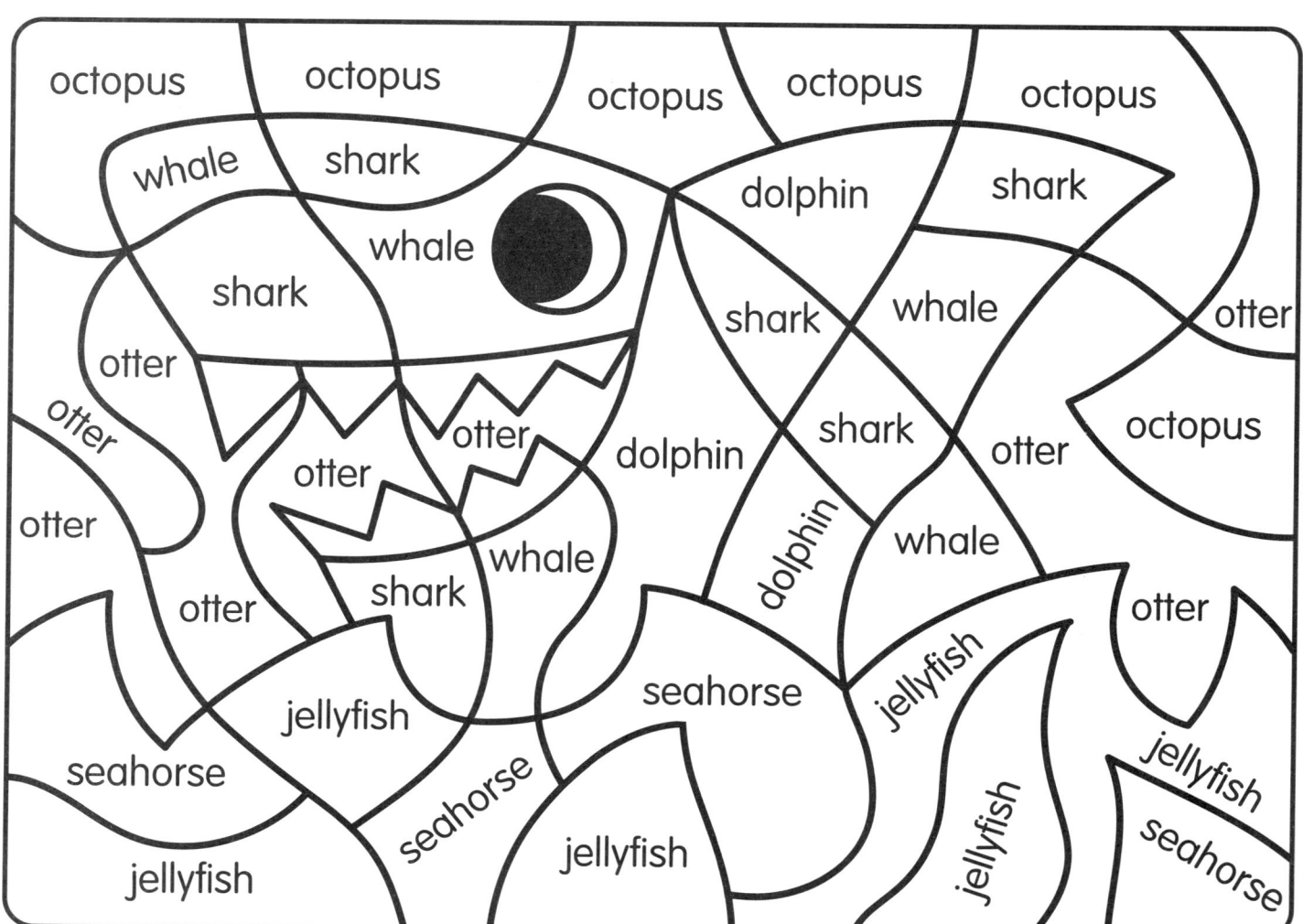

What animal is in the picture? _____

IN THE DEEP BLUE SEA

Name _____

Plenty of Fish in the Sea

Look at the picture. Count the animals.
Then write the missing letters for each animal.

I see 7 ____ ____abs.

I see 5 seah____ ____ses.

I see 3 o____ ____ers.

I see 2 dol____ ____ins.

I see 1 octo____ ____ ____.

crab
dolphin
octopus
otter
seahorse

(IN THE DEEP BLUE SEA)

Name _____

Feeling Crabby

Color the crabs that are holding a compound word.

otter

whale

dolphin

seahorse

shark

jellyfish

Which compound word ends with **sh**?

IN THE DEEP BLUE SEA   Name _____

See the Sea Puzzle

Cut out the puzzle pieces on page 86.
Find the correct piece to finish spelling each word. Glue it.

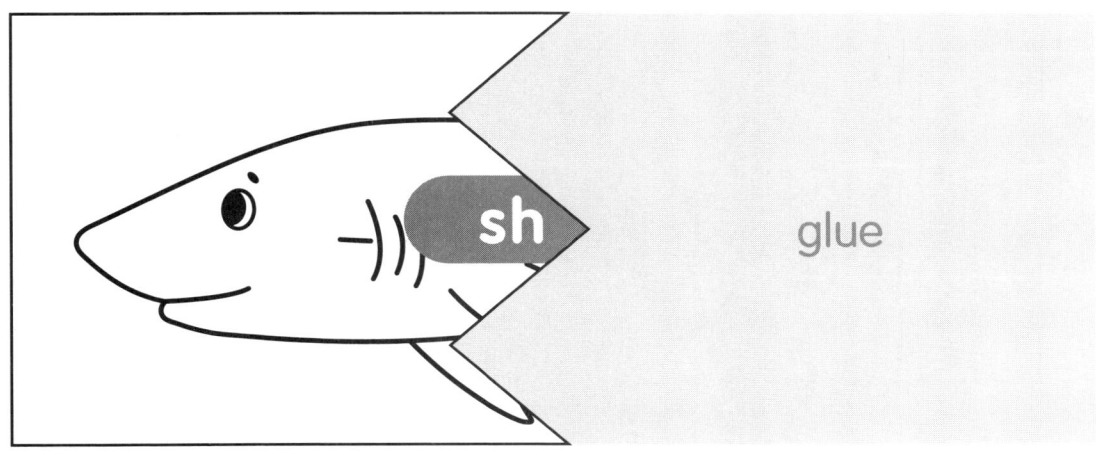

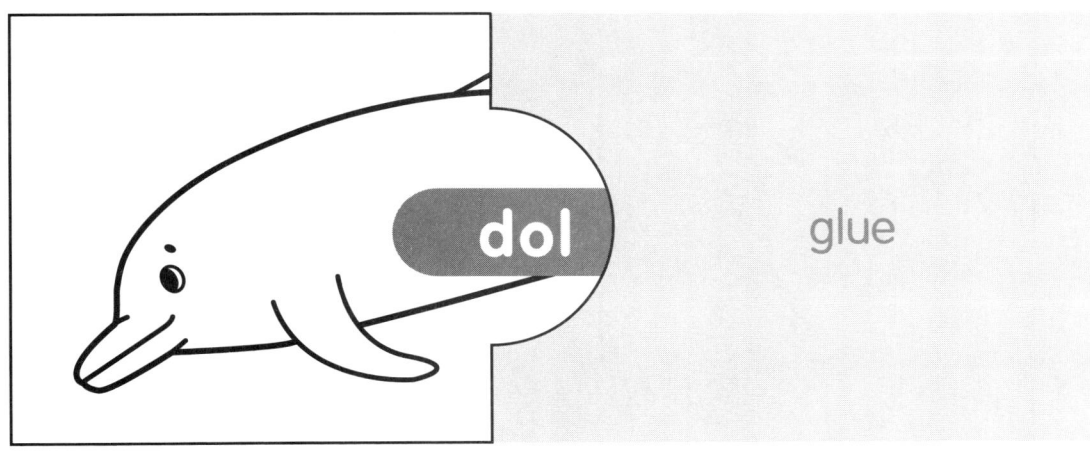

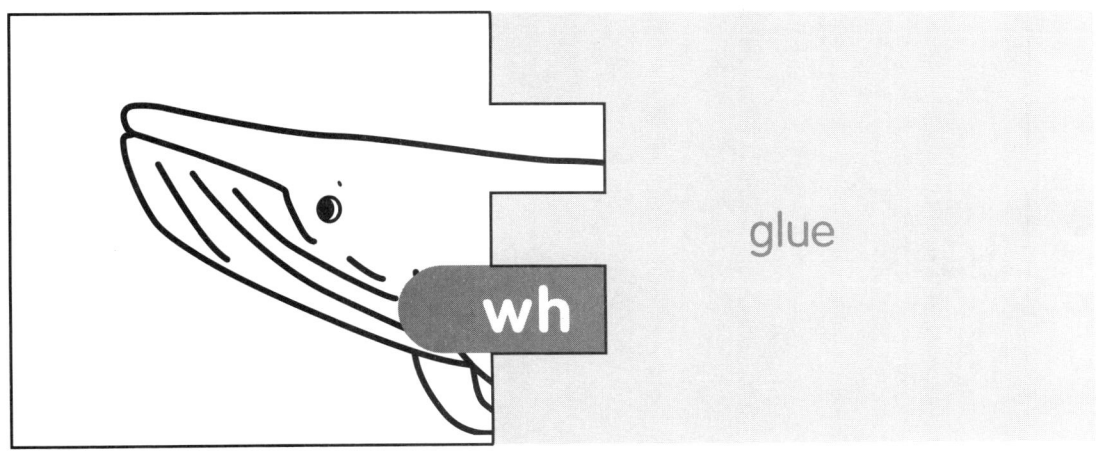

See the Sea Puzzle Cutouts

IN THE DEEP BLUE SEA

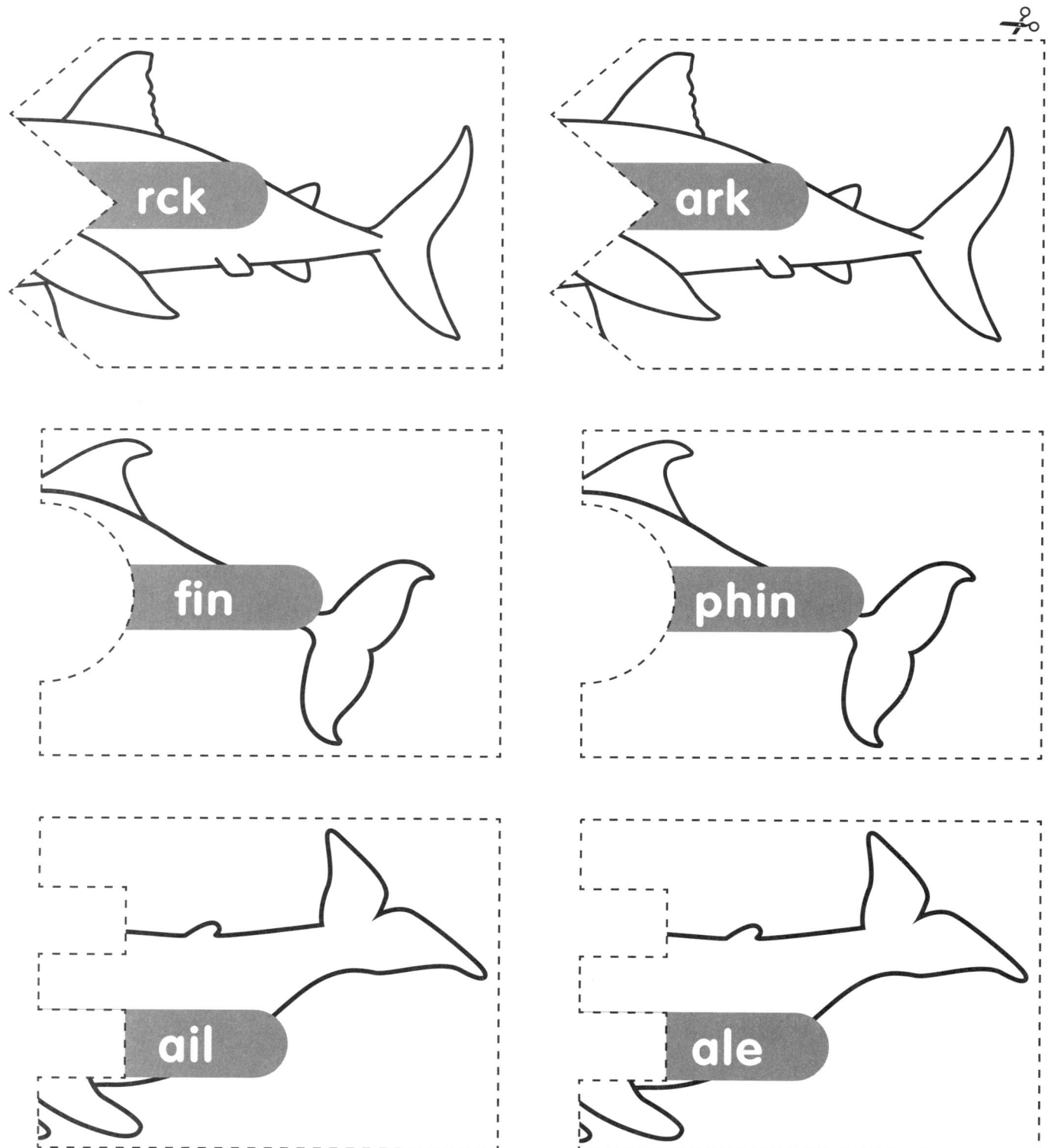

(IN THE DEEP BLUE SEA) Name _____

School of Fish

Help the fish get to their class. Read the class name under each fish.
Then draw a line to match the name to the clue.

seahorse

crab

whale

otter

begins with **wh**

has double letters

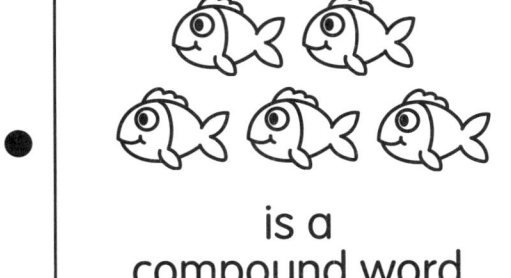
is a compound word

begins with **cr**

IN THE DEEP BLUE SEA

Ocean Animal Shapes

Students have fun using their creativity and spelling words to make an ocean animal with shapes.

What You Need

- In the Deep Blue Sea spelling word list on page 81
- Animal Shape Cutouts on page 89
- What Animal Is It? on page 90
- scissors
- pencil

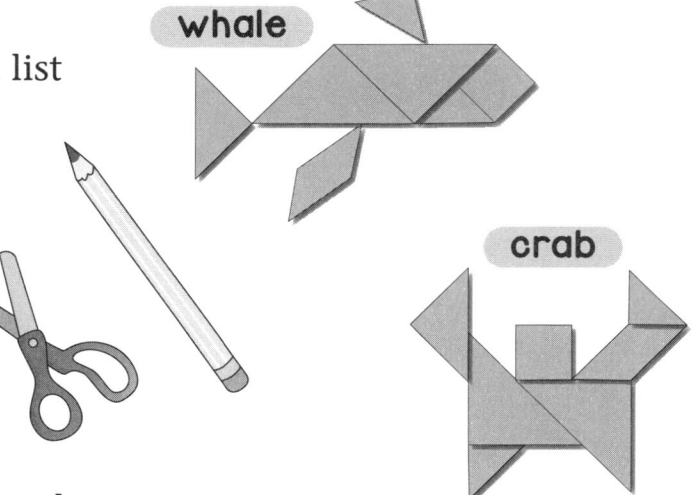

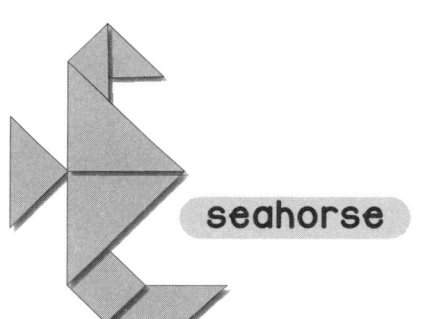

What You Do

1. Print a copy of the spelling word list, the Animal Shape Cutouts, and What Animal Is It? for each student.

2. Distribute the pages along with scissors and a pencil to each student. Then put students in pairs.

3. Have students cut out the shapes.

4. Explain to students that they will use the shapes to create a picture that looks like one of their spelling words. Their partner will try to guess what it is.

5. Have both students in each pair use the shapes to make a picture that represents one of the spelling words. When both students have finished, they will look at their partner's picture and guess which ocean animal it is. They will write their guess on the What Animal Is It? sheet. Then students will tell their partners which spelling word is shown in the picture, and the students will write down the correct answer. Have the students do this three times.

IN THE DEEP BLUE SEA

Animal Shape Cutouts

IN THE DEEP BLUE SEA

What Animal Is It?

Write to tell what you guess your partner made.
Then write what your partner answers.

| seahorse | crab | shark | dolphin |
| jellyfish | otter | whale | octopus |

	Guesses	Answers
1		
2		
3		

Extra Practice Worksheets

This section provides an additional 197 words to give students even more practice with spelling patterns and word study! The activity pages can be used independently or to enhance *Building Spelling Skills* weekly lessons.

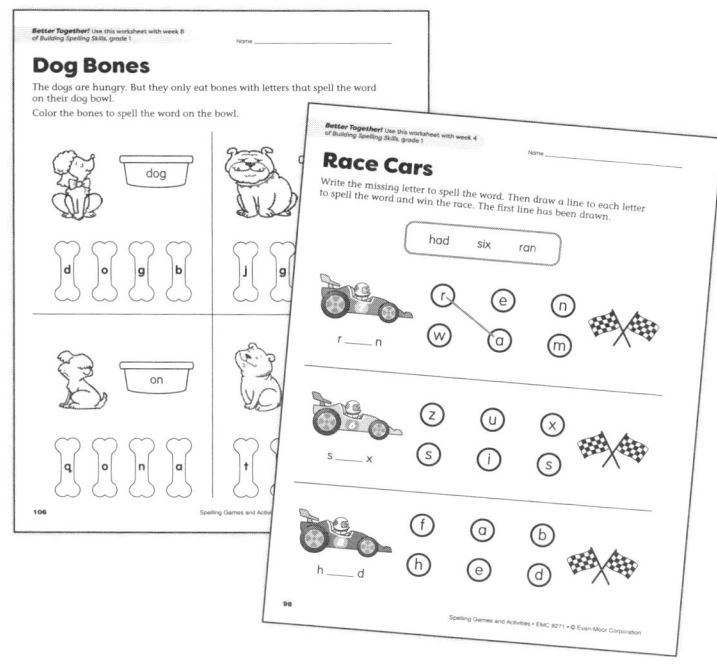

Better Together!

The worksheets in this section correspond to each week in *Building Spelling Skills*, grade 1.

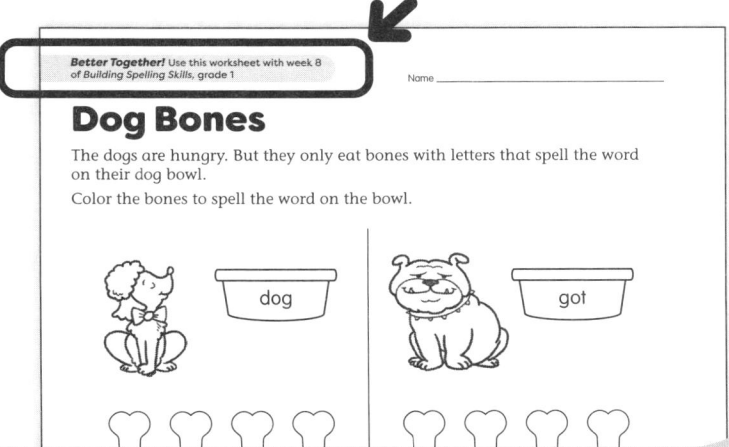

Better Together! Use this worksheet with week 1 of *Building Spelling Skills*, grade 1

Name _____

Apples for Alligators

The alligators are hungry. But they only eat apples with letters that spell the word on their shirt.

Color the apples to spell the word on the alligator's shirt.

Better Together! Use this worksheet with week 1 of *Building Spelling Skills*, grade 1

Name _____

Hidden at the Park

Find 5 words at the pond. Circle them.
Then write the words you found.

1. ___ ___

2. ___ ___

3. ___ ___

4. ___

5. ___ ___ ___

Better Together! Use this worksheet with week 2 of *Building Spelling Skills*, grade 1

Name _____

Baby Birds

Help the daddy bird find his baby birds.
Color the birds that match the words from the box.

| in | is | it | big | did |

 im

 it

 bib

 at

 big

 is

 did

 dig

 in

Better Together! Use this worksheet with week 2 of *Building Spelling Skills*, grade 1

Name _____

Bird Foods

Unscramble the letters on each bird to spell a word.
Then cut and glue the food with the same word to feed the bird.

Bird	Word		Food
ni	_____	glue	it
gbi	_____	glue	did
ti	_____	glue	is
si	_____	glue	in
ddi	_____	glue	big

© Evan-Moor Corporation • EMC 8271 • Spelling Games and Activities

Better Together! Use this worksheet with week 3 of *Building Spelling Skills*, grade 1

Name _____

Write About It!

Finish the sentence about the picture using the words from the box. You can use a word more than one time.

> can   cat   man   pan   sat

A ___ ___ ___ eats food from a ___ ___ ___ .

The ___ ___ ___ cooks food in a ___ ___ ___ .

The ___ ___ ___ loves his pet ___ ___ ___ .

The ___ ___ ___ ___ ___ ___ on the mat.

Which Letter?

Write the missing letter to finish spelling the word.
Circle the child who has the missing letter.

> can   cat   man   pan

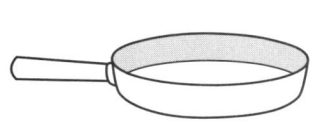

p ___ n

ca ___

___ at

m ___ n

Race Cars

Write the missing letter to spell the word. Then draw a line to each letter to spell the word and win the race. The first line has been drawn.

had   six   ran

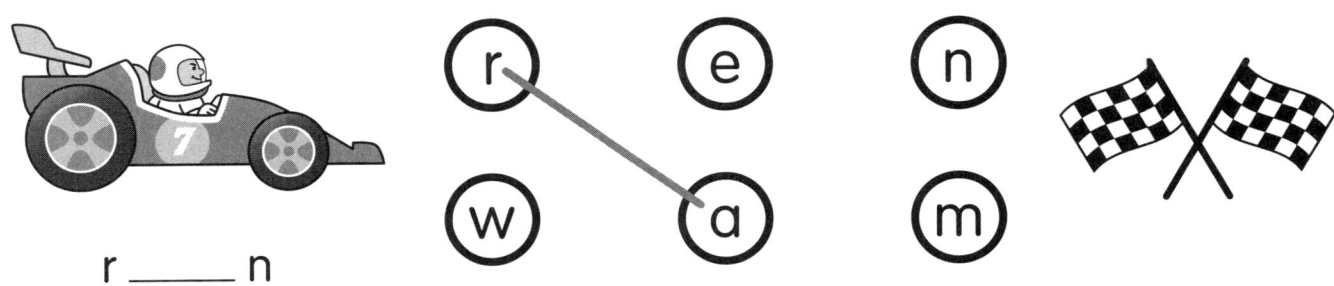

r ___ n

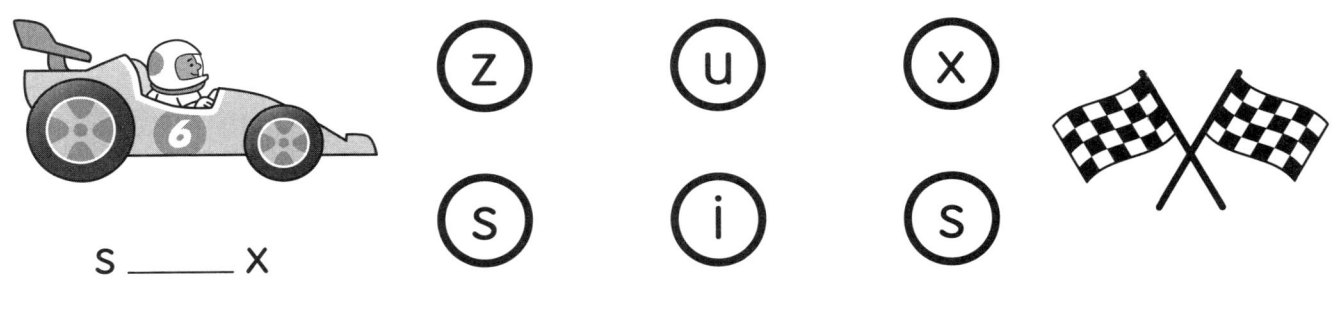

s ___ x

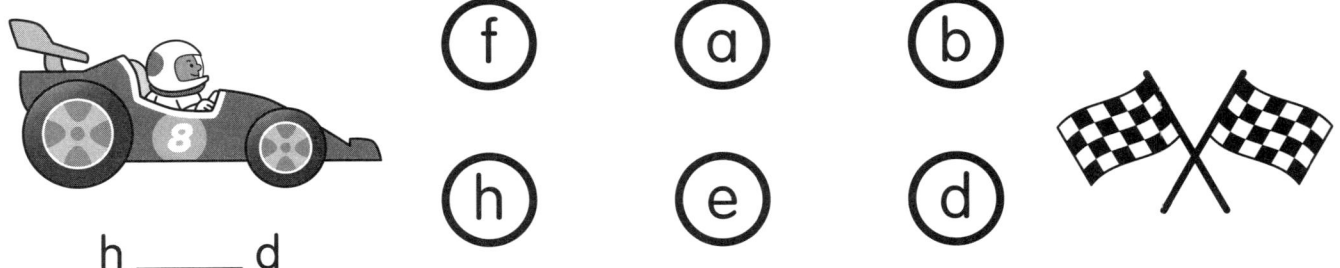

h ___ d

Car Shop

Help fix the cars. Cut and glue the car parts onto the correct car.

Lion Cubs

Help the lion find his cubs. Color the cubs that match the words from the box.

| up | us | run | fun | to |

too

two

to

fun

tug

us

run

up

Better Together! Use this worksheet with week 5 of *Building Spelling Skills*, grade 1

Name _____

Feed the Seals

Unscramble the letters on each seal to spell a word.
Then cut and glue the fish with the same word to feed the seal.

Seal	Word	Glue
pu	_____	glue
urn	_____	glue
su	_____	glue
nuf	_____	glue
ot	_____	glue

Fish:
- fun
- run
- to
- us
- up

Write About It!

Finish the sentence about the picture using the words from the box.
Use each word one time.

> pup   bus   I   tub   but

He likes bananas, _____
he likes apples more.

_____ play with my _____.

We ride on the _____.

He is in the _____.

Better Together! Use this worksheet with week 6 of *Building Spelling Skills*, grade 1

Name _____

Balloon Pop

Write the missing letter to finish spelling the word.
Color the balloon that has the missing letter.

pup   bus   tub   but

b____s	i	a	u	e
tu____	p	b	d	n
p____p	i	e	a	u
____ut	b	g	h	d

Better Together! Use this worksheet with week 7 of *Building Spelling Skills*, grade 1

Name _____

The Way Home

Help the cookie get back to its house. Write the word for each step.

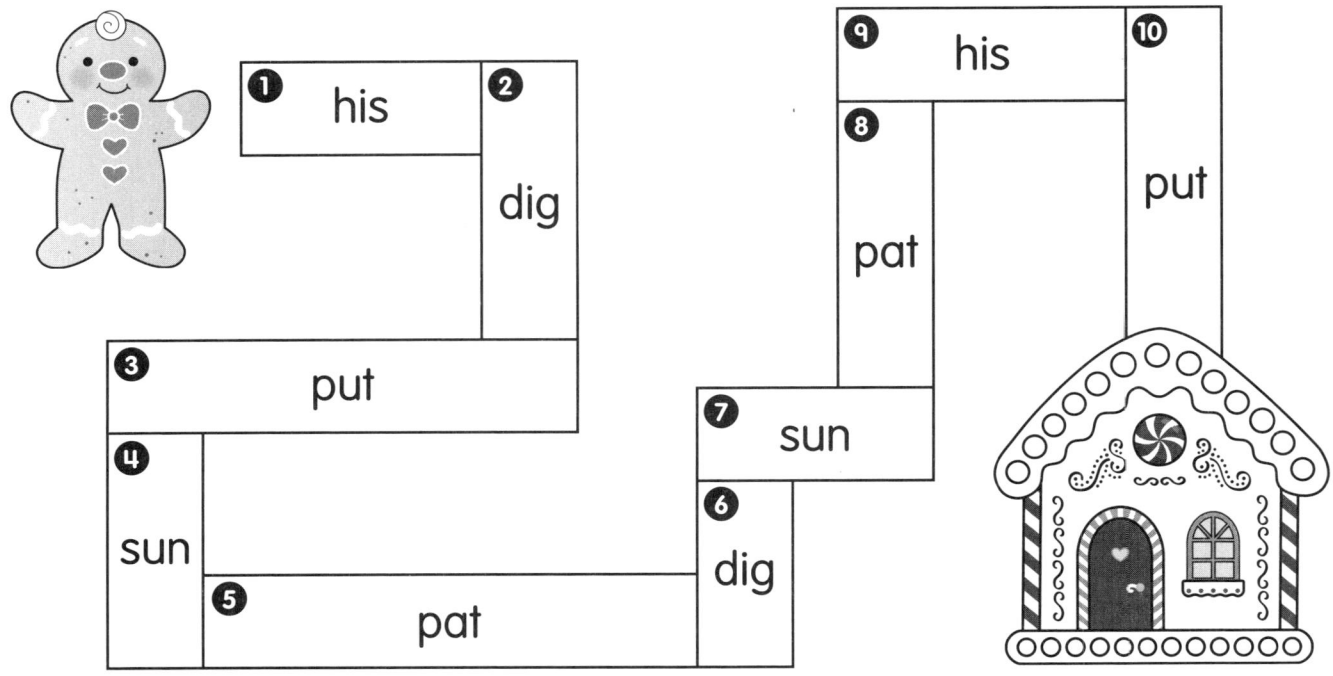

Step ❶ ➡ _____his_____	Step ❻ ⬆ _____
Step ❷ ⬇ _____	Step ❼ ➡ _____
Step ❸ ⬅ _____	Step ❽ ⬆ _____
Step ❹ ⬇ _____	Step ❾ ➡ _____
Step ❺ ➡ _____	Step ❿ ⬇ _____

Unscramble and Solve

Unscramble the letters to write a word from the box.

> dig   pat   sun   put

tup ___ ___ ___
     1

atp ___ ___ ___
     2   5

gid ___ ___ ___
         3

snu ___ ___ ___
             4

Now write the numbered letters in the matching spaces to answer the riddle.

What is Nadia's favorite thing to do?

1 2 3 4 5

Dog Bones

The dogs are hungry. But they only eat bones with letters that spell the word on their dog bowl.

Color the bones to spell the word on the bowl.

In the Doghouse

Find 5 words in the yard. Circle them.
Then write the words you found.

1. _____

2. _____

3. _____

4. _____

5. _____

Better Together! Use this worksheet with week 9 of *Building Spelling Skills*, grade 1

Name _____

Baby Pandas

Help the panda mom find her babies.
Circle the pandas that match the words from the box.

| pet   get   let   fed   red |

Fish Food

Unscramble the letters on each fish to spell a word.
Then cut and glue the worm with the same word to feed the fish.

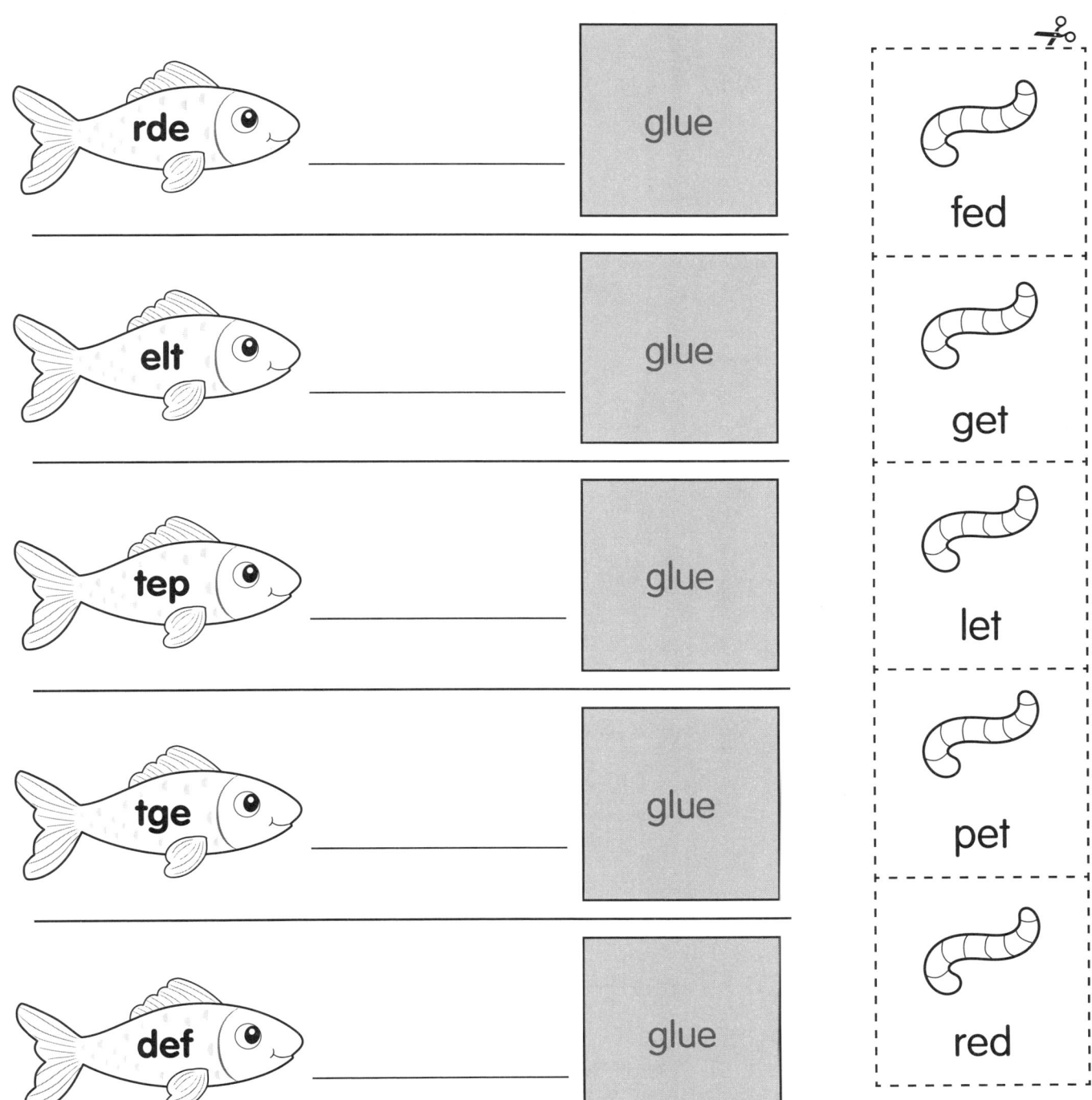

Maze of Short Sounds

Help the fox get to the box.
Follow the words with a short vowel sound.

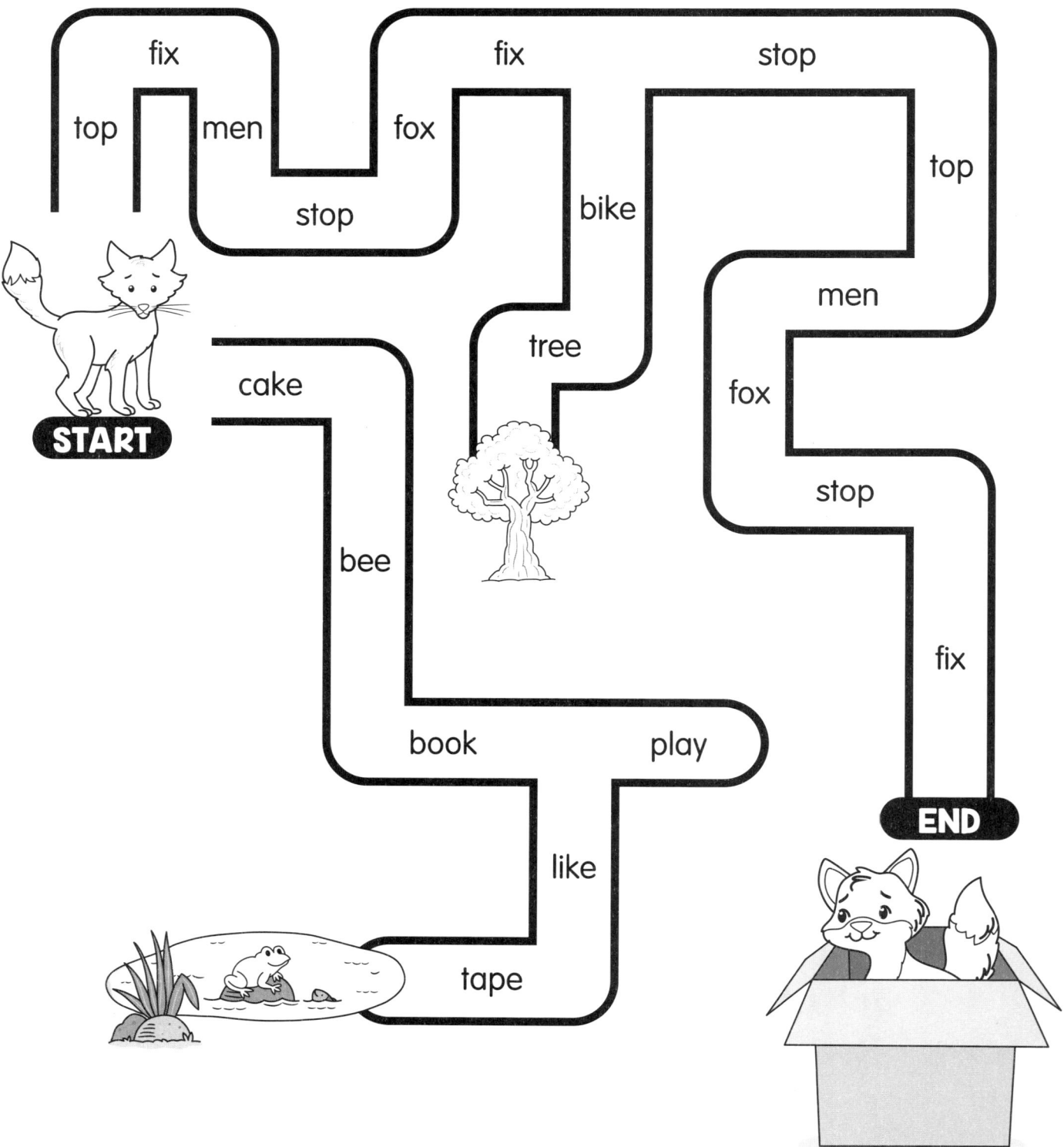

Clues and a Riddle

Read each clue and write a spelling word to answer it.

stop   men   fix   fox

A ☐☐☐ is an animal that lives in the forest.

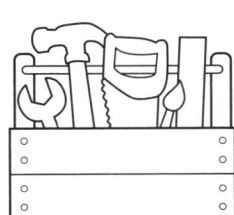

If something is broken, you can 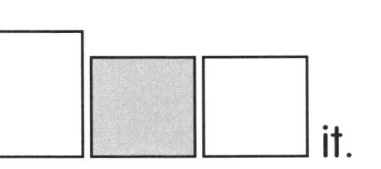 it.

Boys grow up to be ☐☐☐.

Cars 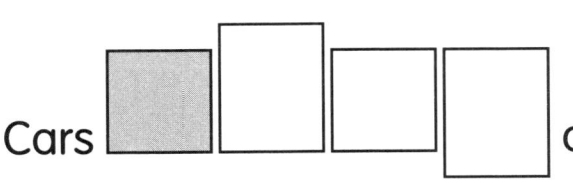 at a red light.

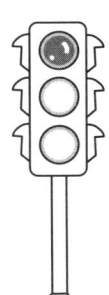

Now write the letters from the gray boxes in order to solve the riddle.

What do fish have that help them swim?

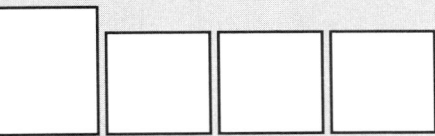

Better Together! Use this worksheet with week 11 of *Building Spelling Skills*, grade 1

Name _____

Hen Eggs

Help the hen find her eggs. Her eggs have the same letters as the word on her feathers.

Color the eggs to spell the word on each hen.

 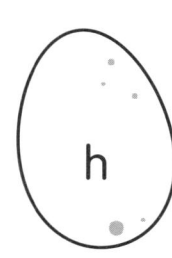 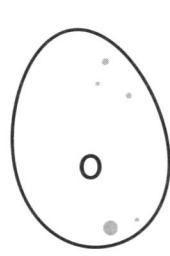 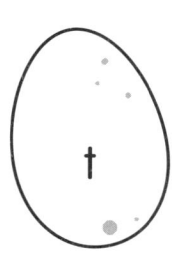 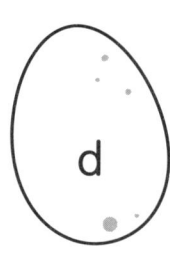 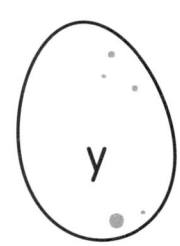

hot — h o t d y

 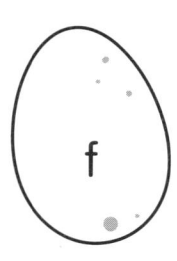 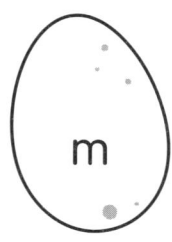 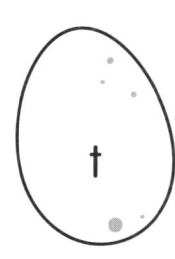 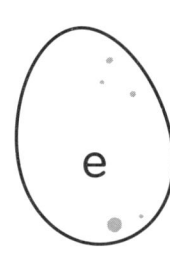 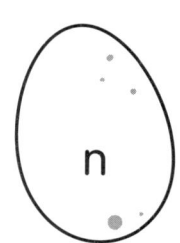

ten — f m t e n

 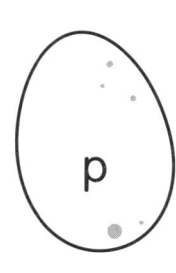 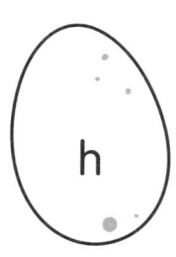 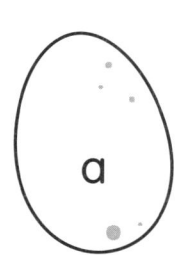 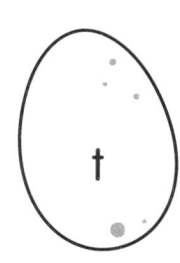 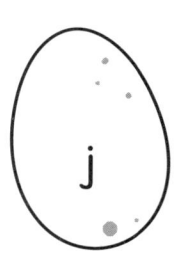

hat — p h a t j

 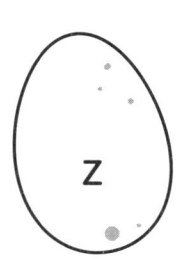 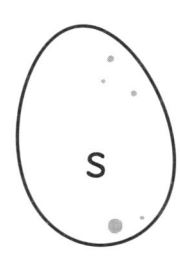 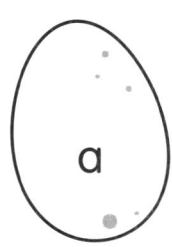 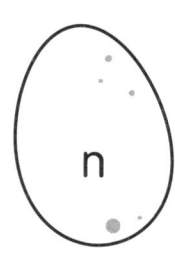 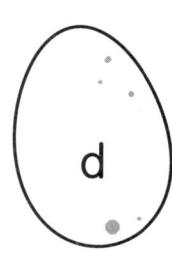

sand — z s a n d

Hidden at the Beach

Find 5 words at the beach. Circle them.
Then write the words you found.

1. _____ _____ _____
2. _____ _____ _____
3. _____ _____ _____
4. _____ _____ _____
5. _____ _____ _____

One More Drawing

Draw one more. Then write a word from the box that tells about the picture.

> pigs   cats   beds   tops   bugs

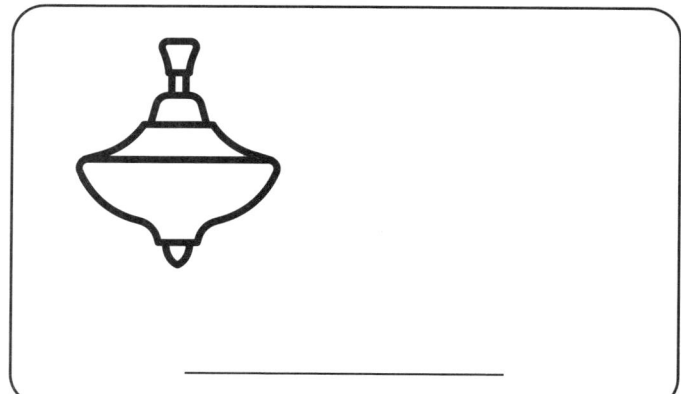

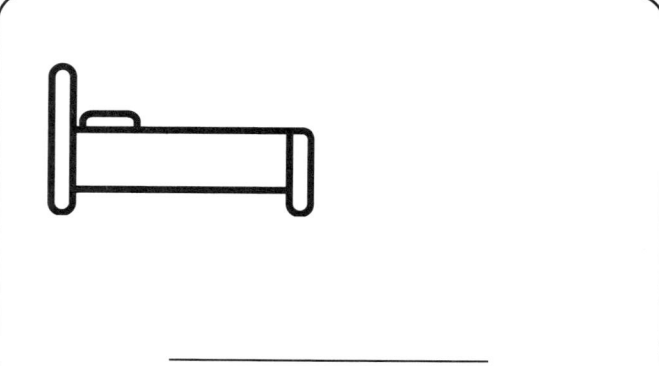

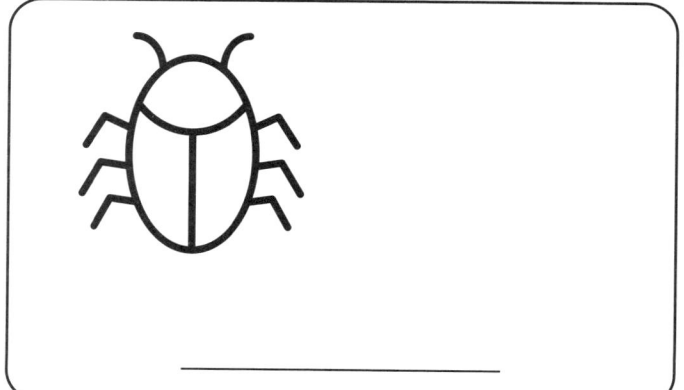

Word Scramble

Unscramble the letters to write a word.
Then draw a line to match the word to a picture.

pigs   cats   beds   tops   bugs

sdeb _____ •   •

asct _____ •   •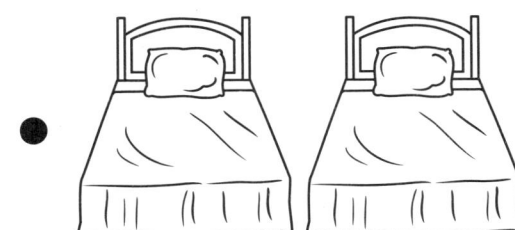

ipsg _____ •   •

pots _____ •   •

gubs _____ •   •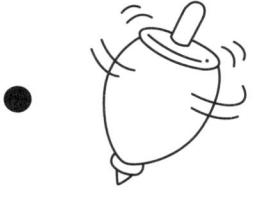

Better Together! Use this worksheet with week 13 of *Building Spelling Skills*, grade 1

Name _____

Butterflies

Help each butterfly get to a flower by following a spelling word. Color the squares to spell the word. Look at the example.

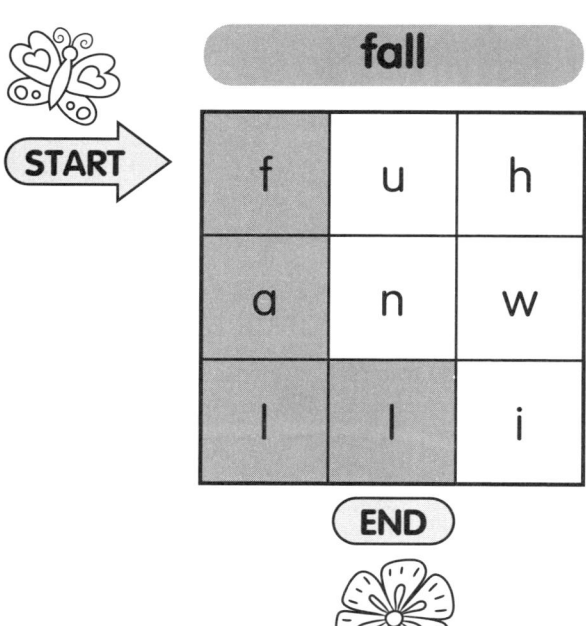

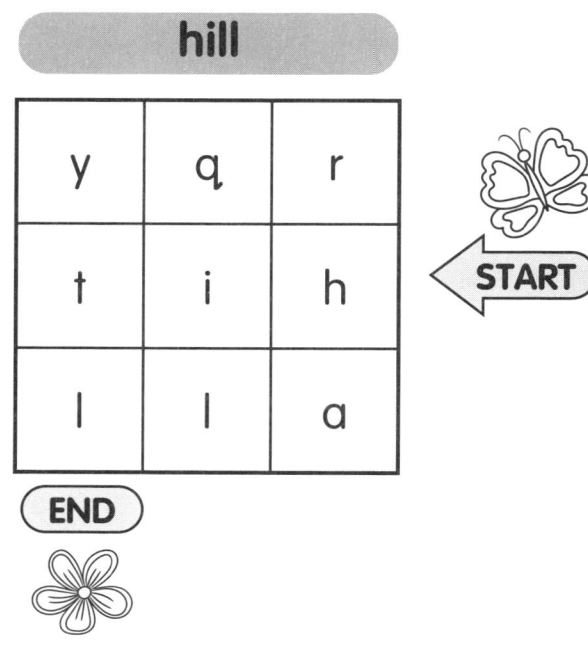

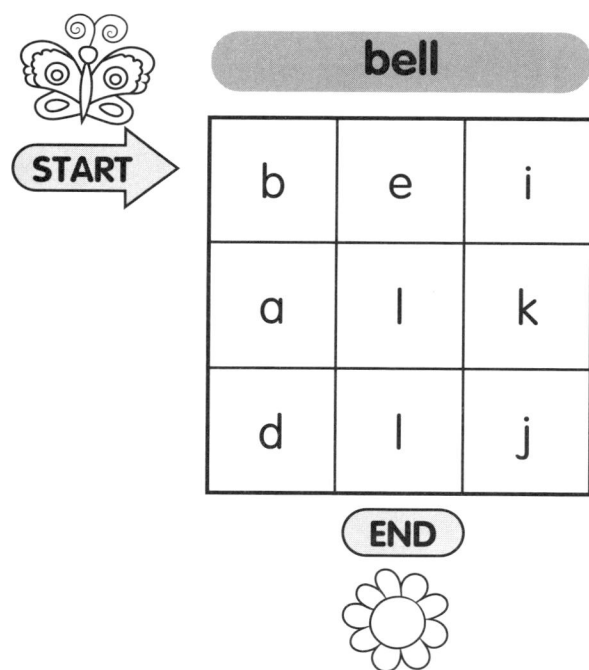

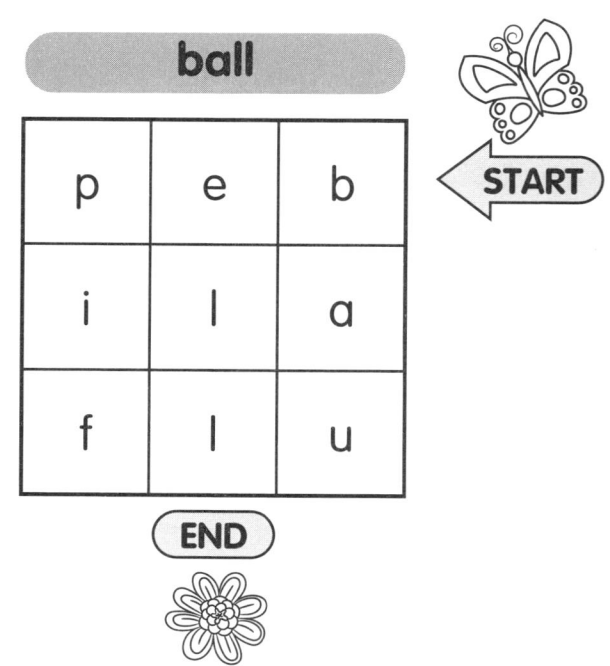

Better Together! Use this worksheet with week 13 of *Building Spelling Skills*, grade 1

Name _____

Secret Sentences

Use the secret code to write a spelling word. Match each shape in the word to a letter.

Example

We ran up the <u>h</u> <u>i</u> <u>l</u> <u>l</u>.
♥ △ ○ ○

Do you want to play with the ___ ___ ___ ___?
🌀 ☐ ○ ○

I ring the ___ ___ ___ ___.
🌀 ☆ ○ ○

The apple ___ ___ ___ ___ off the tree.
◇ ☆ ○ ○

Did you ___ ___ ___ ___ off your bike?
◇ ☐ ○ ○

© Evan-Moor Corporation • EMC 8271 • Spelling Games and Activities

117

Better Together! Use this worksheet with week 14 of *Building Spelling Skills*, grade 1

Name _____

Basketball Teams

Read the flags.
Then read the word below each player.
Cut and glue each word below the correct flag.

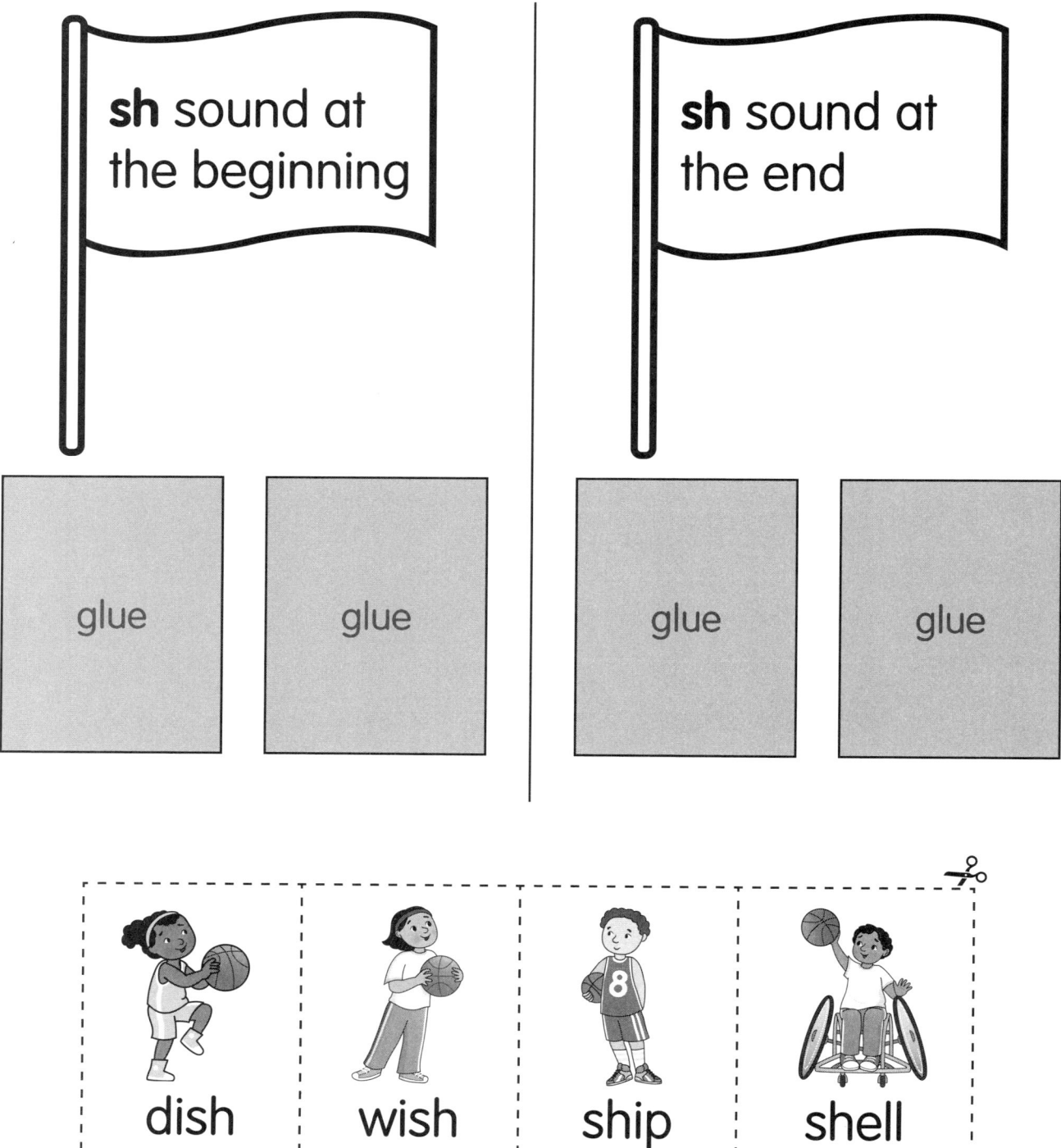

Missing at School

Write the missing letter to finish spelling the word.
Cross off each letter after you use it.

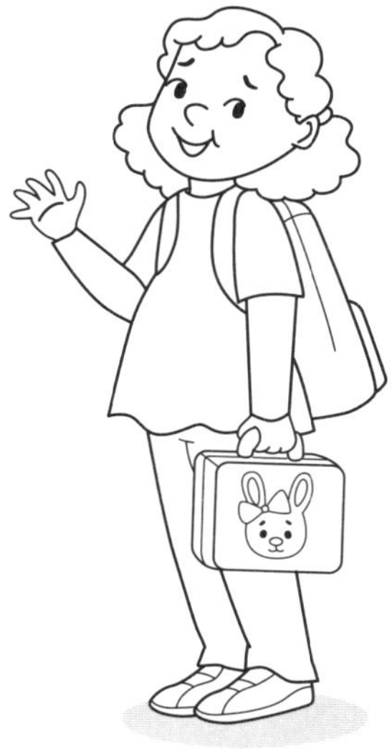

h　　e　　d　　s　　i

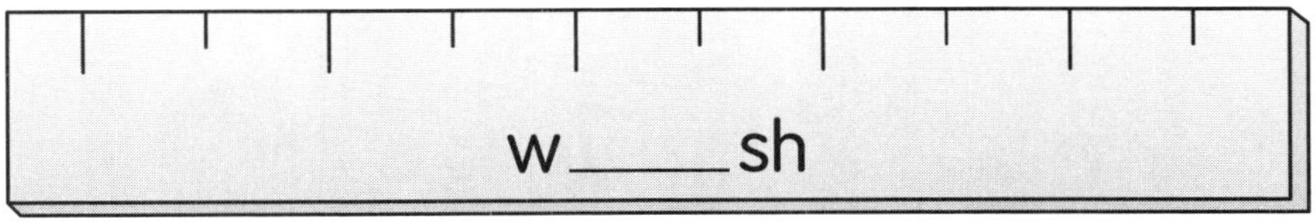

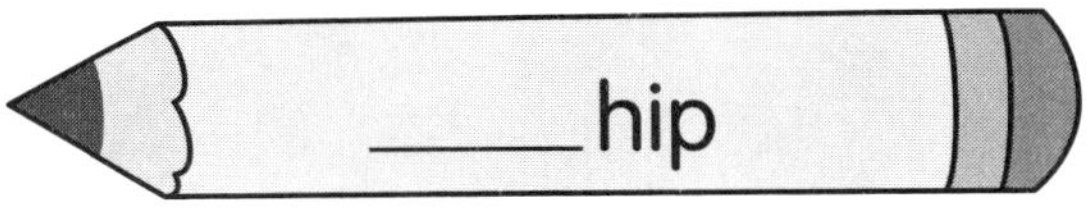

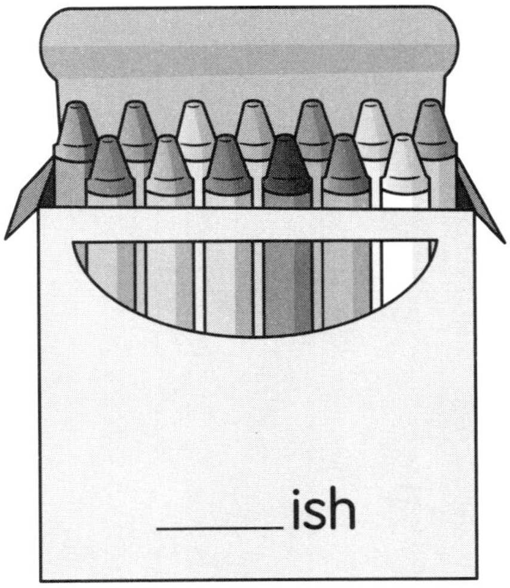

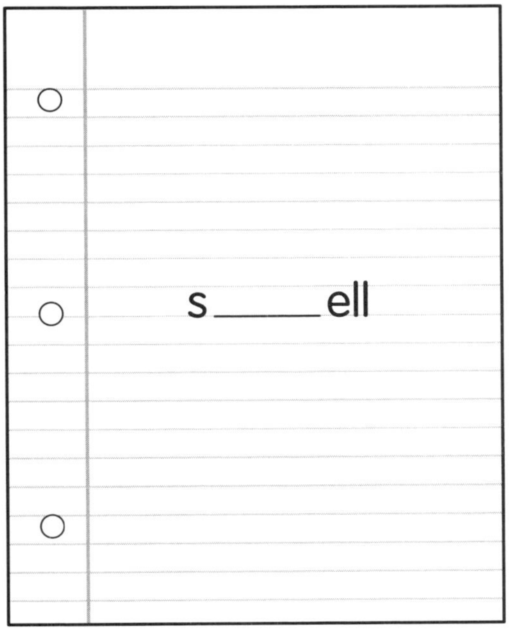

w____sh

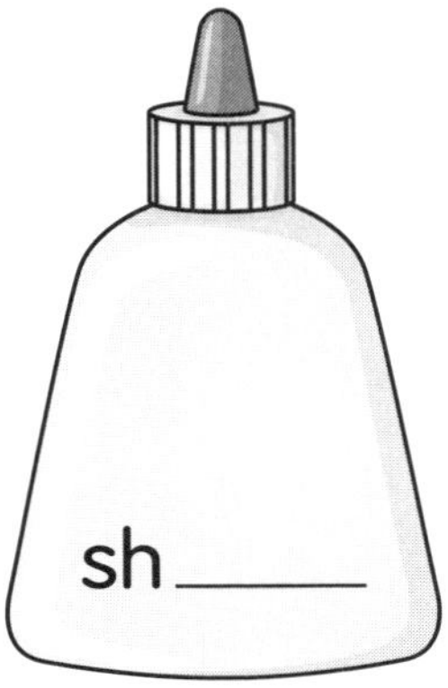

____hip

sh____

____ish

s____ell

| dish | she | shell | ship | wish |

Better Together! Use this worksheet with week 15 of *Building Spelling Skills*, grade 1

Name _____

Ape Maze

Help the ape get to the grapes.
Follow the words with a **long a** sound.

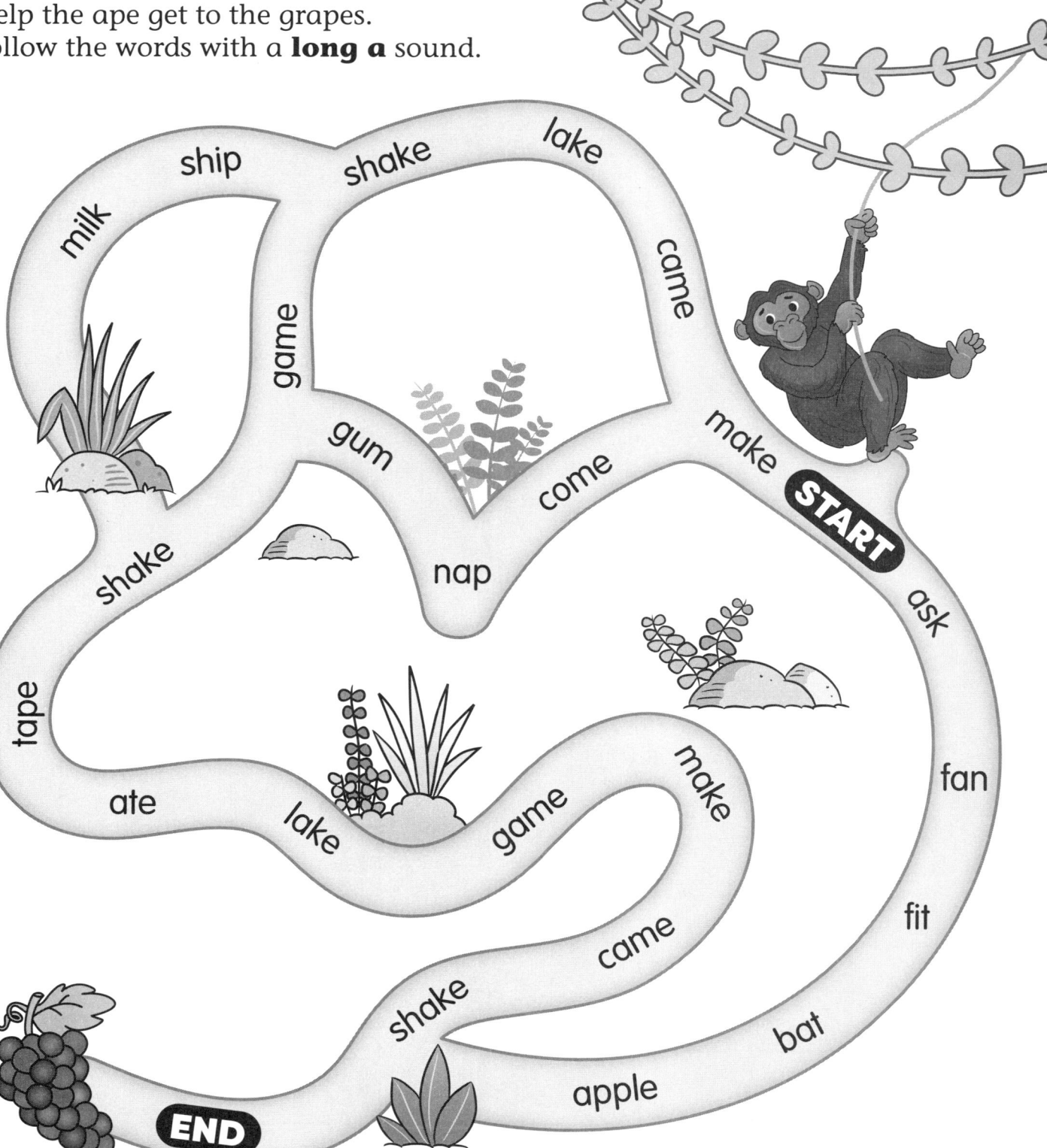

Better Together! Use this worksheet with week 15 of *Building Spelling Skills*, grade 1

Name _____

Clues and a Riddle

Read each clue and write a spelling word to answer it.

> make   came   lake   game   shake   ate   tape   come

move back and forth   ☐ ☐ ☐ ☐ ☐

a place to swim   ☐ ☐ ☐ ☐

something you play   ☐ ☐ ☐ ☐

sticky stuff   ☐ ☐ ☐ ☐

had lunch   ☐ ☐ ☐

Now write the letters from the gray boxes in order to solve the riddle.

With my special shoes I will go for a ride,
On the sidewalk I'll roll, and on the ice I'll glide.

What does the boy want to do?

☐ ☐ ☐ ☐ ☐

Better Together! Use this worksheet with week 16 of *Building Spelling Skills*, grade 1

Name _____

Find the Treasure

Help the pirate get to the treasure.
Write the word for each step.

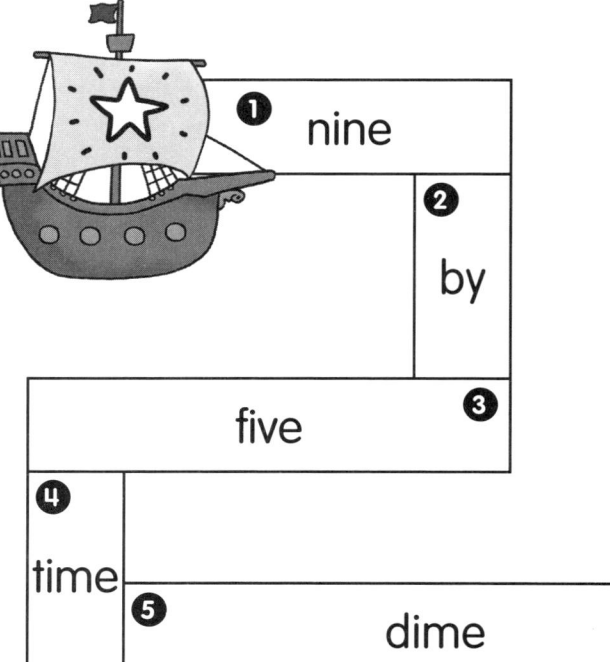
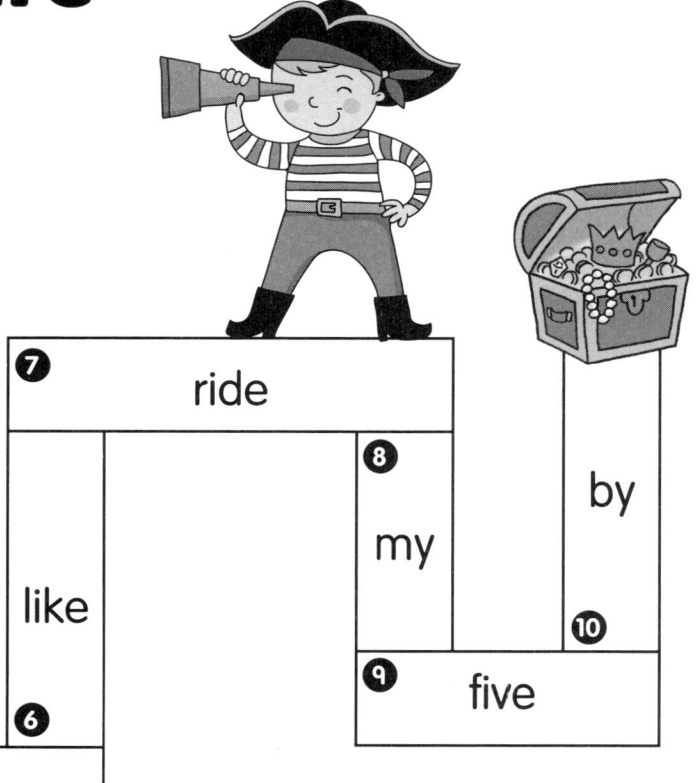

Step ❶ →	nine	Step ❻ ↑	_____
Step ❷ ↓	_____	Step ❼ →	_____
Step ❸ ←	_____	Step ❽ ↓	_____
Step ❹ ↓	_____	Step ❾ →	_____
Step ❺ →	_____	Step ❿ ↑	_____

Unscramble and Solve

Unscramble the letters to write a word from the box.

> ride   five   dime   like   nine

nein __ __ __ __
            5

fevi __ __ __ __
         3 4

mide __ __ __ __
      1

dier __ __ __ __
         2

Now write the numbered letters in the matching spaces to answer the riddle.

What does Lewis like to do?

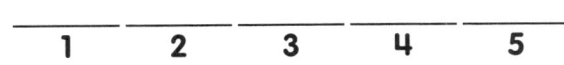
 1 2 3 4 5

Better Together! Use this worksheet with week 17 of *Building Spelling Skills*, grade 1

Name _____

Blast Off!

Write the missing letters to spell the word. Then draw a line to each letter to spell the word and get to the planet. The first line has been drawn.

rake   fine   bike

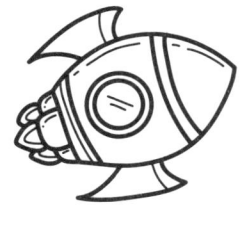

f ___ n ___

r ___ k ___

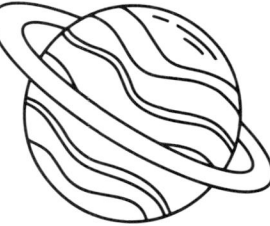

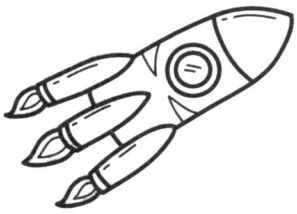

b ___ k ___

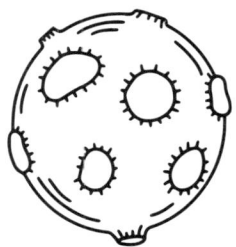

Spelling Games and Activities • EMC 8271 • © Evan-Moor Corporation

Better Together! Use this worksheet with week 17 of *Building Spelling Skills*, grade 1

Name _____

Candy Jars

Help put the candies away.
Cut and glue the candies onto the correct jar.

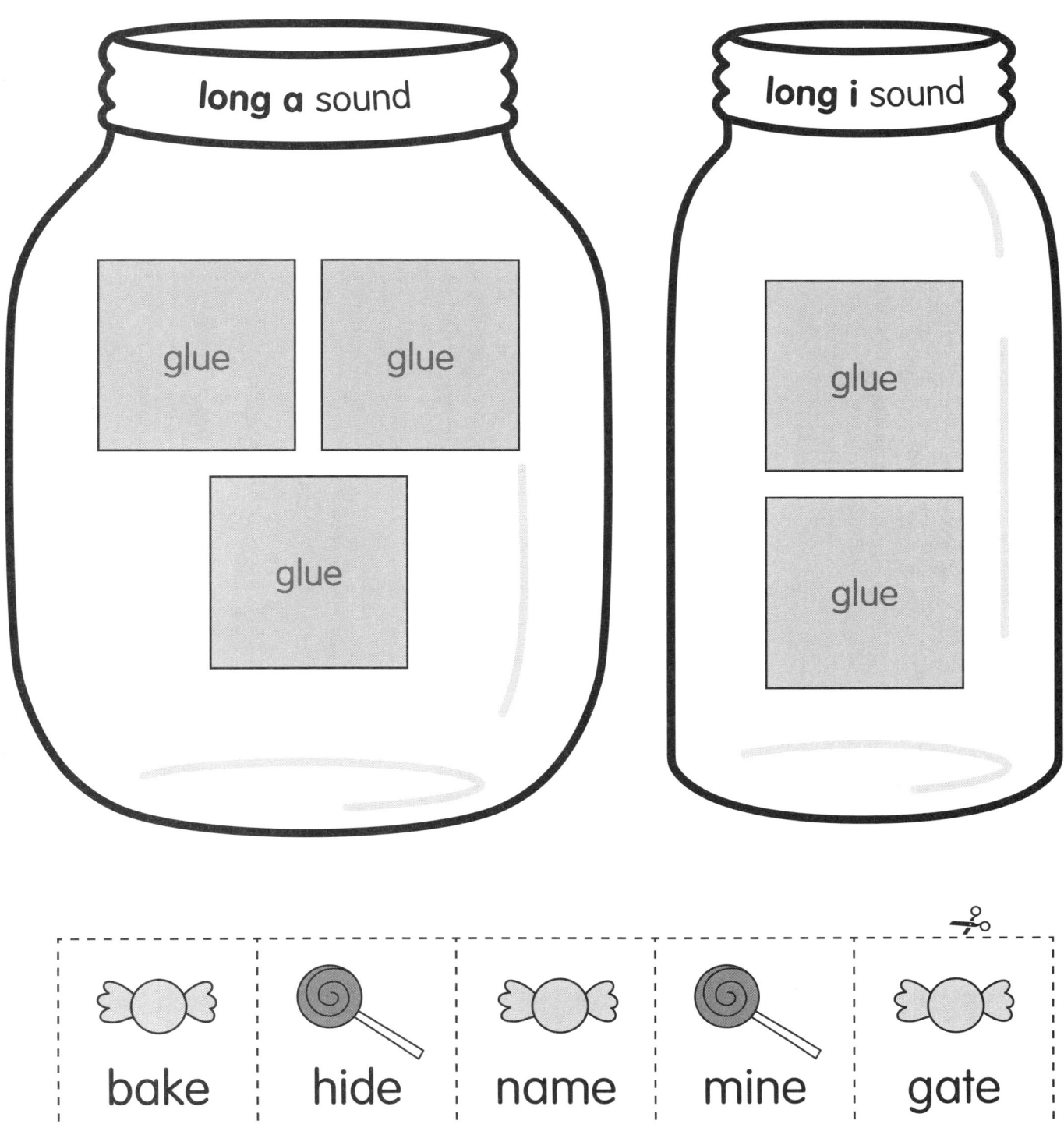

Little Lambs

Help the sheep find her baby lambs.
Color the lambs that match the words from the box.

| we | me | he | be | see | need | tree | sheep |

Snack Time

Unscramble the letters above each child to spell a word.
Then cut and glue the snack with the same word to feed the child.

ees _____ glue

eb _____ glue

eret _____ glue

eden _____ glue

ew _____ glue

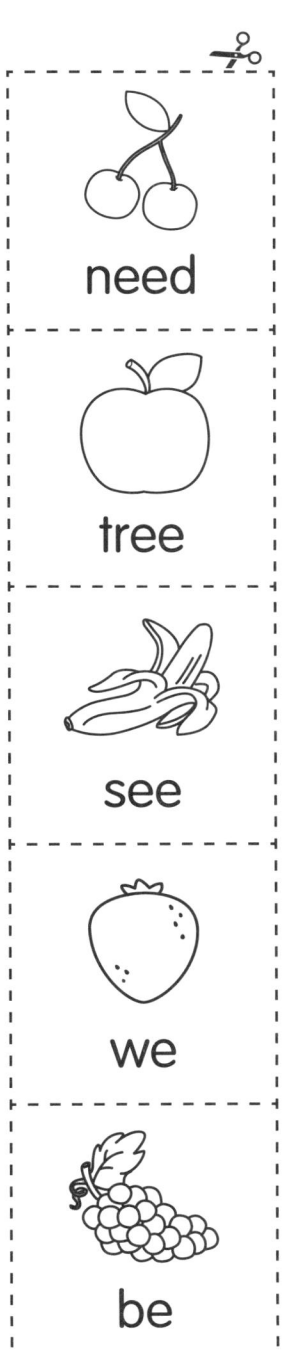

need

tree

see

we

be

Better Together! Use this worksheet with week 19 of *Building Spelling Skills,* grade 1

Name _____

Pot of Gold

Help each leprechaun get to the pot of gold by following a spelling word. Color the squares to spell a word. Look at the example.

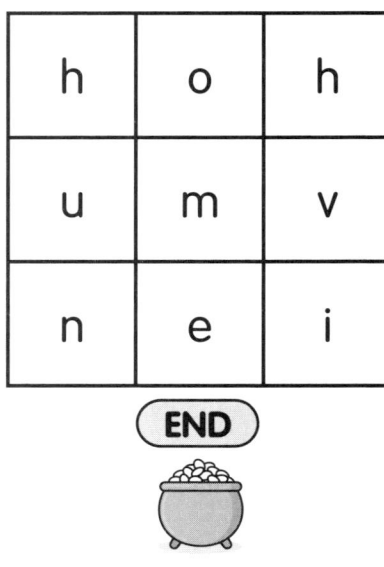

note

n	o	k
f	t	a
c	e	j

START → END

home

h	o	h
u	m	v
n	e	i

START ← END

you

y	u	w
o	e	a
u	q	h

START → END

robe

y	e	r
p	b	o
d	e	w

START ← END

128 Spelling Games and Activities • EMC 8271 • © Evan-Moor Corporation

Better Together! Use this worksheet with week 19 of *Building Spelling Skills*, grade 1

Name _____

Secret Sentences

Use the secret code to write a spelling word. Match each shape in the word to a letter.

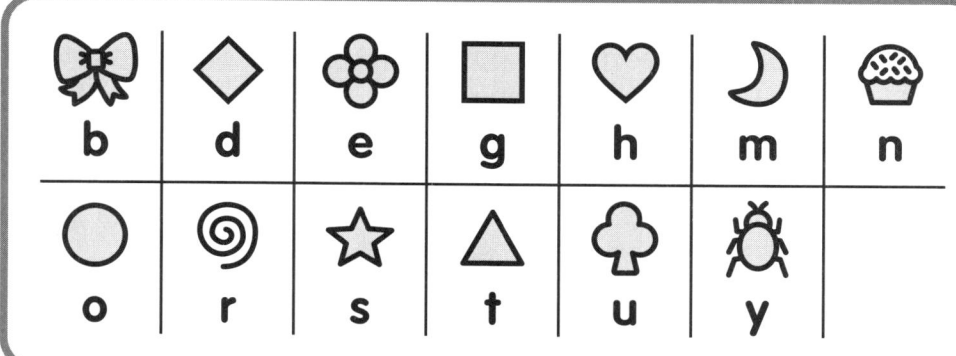

Example

Joy wrote a __n__ __o__ __t__ __e__.

He likes to wear a ____ ____ ____ ____.

What ____ ____ ____ ____ ____ want to eat?

I put on my shoes ____ ____ I can play outside.

I want to ____ ____ ____ ____ ____ ____.

© Evan-Moor Corporation • EMC 8271 • Spelling Games and Activities

Train Ride

Write the missing letters to spell the word. Then draw a line to each letter to spell the word and help the train pick up the people. The first line has been drawn.

gave   cone   line

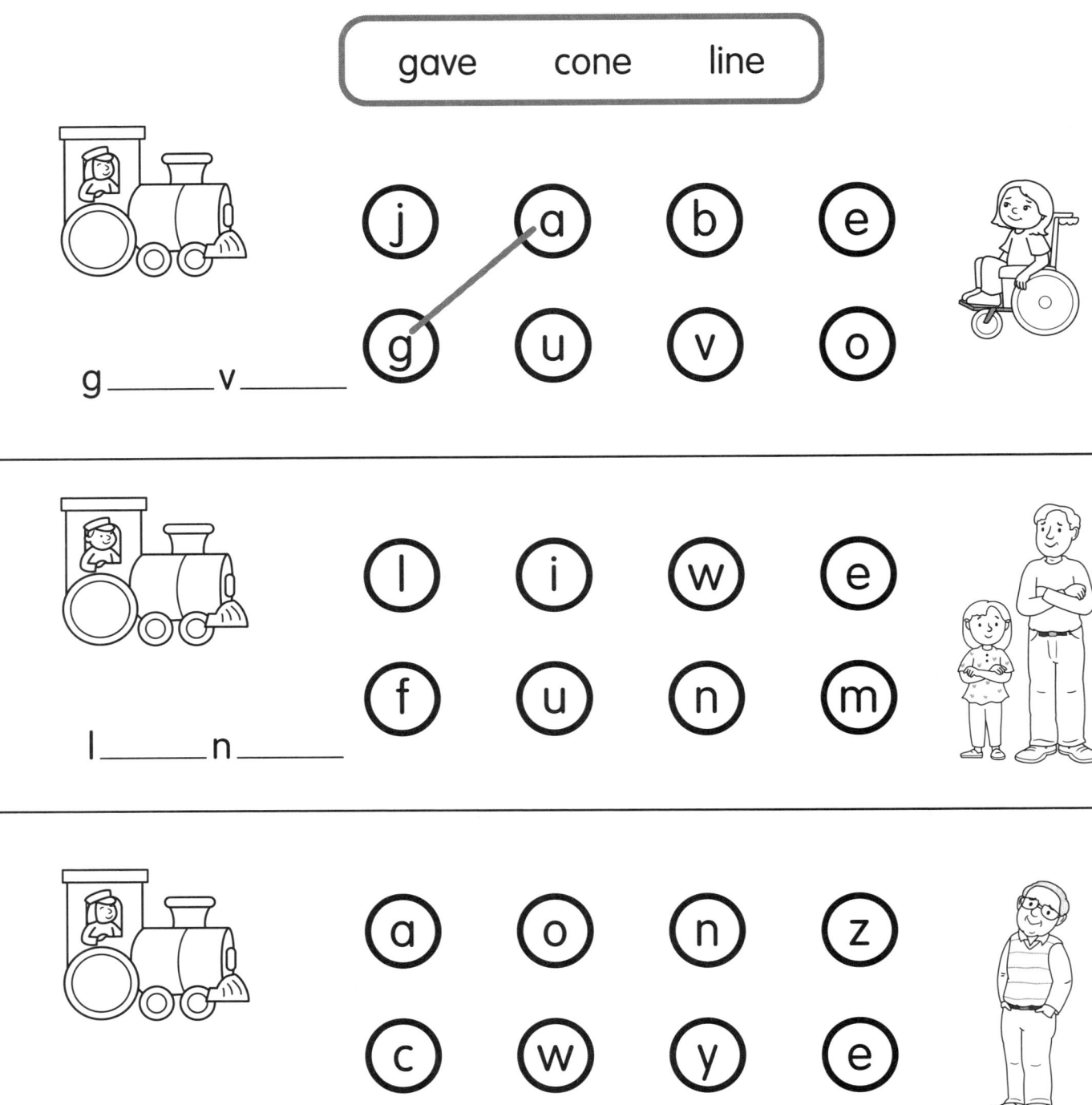

g ___ v ___

l ___ n ___

c ___ n ___

Toy Box

Help put the toys away.
Cut and glue the toys onto the correct toy box.

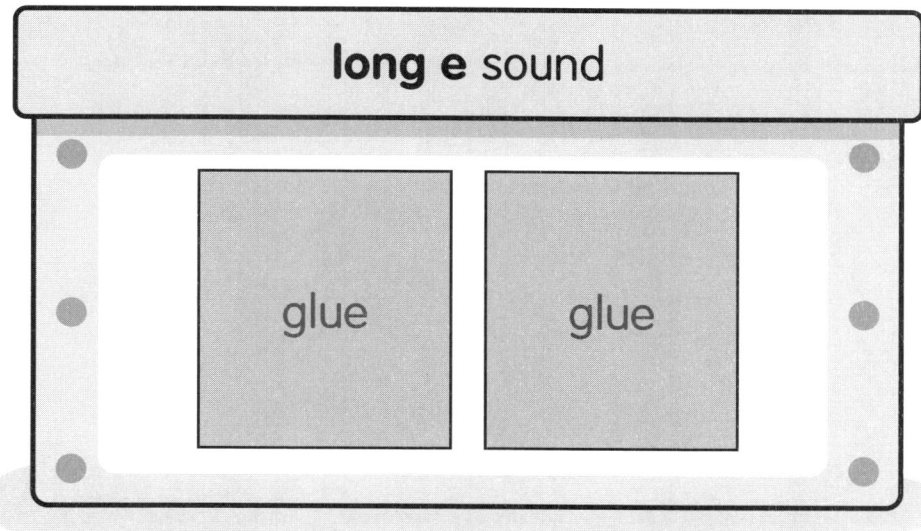

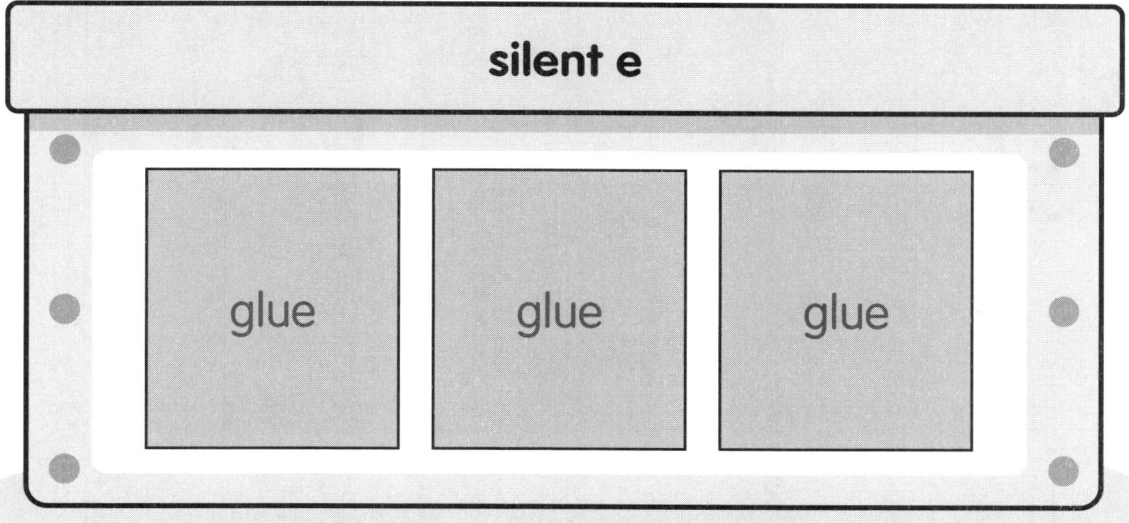

Better Together! Use this worksheet with week 21 of *Building Spelling Skills,* grade 1

Name _____

One More Drawing

Draw one more. Then write a word from the box that tells about the picture.

> bees   boxes   cakes   foxes   kites   roses

_____

_____

_____

_____

_____

_____

Better Together! Use this worksheet with week 21 of *Building Spelling Skills*, grade 1

Name _____

Word Scramble

Unscramble the letters to write a word.
Then draw a line to match the word to a picture.

> bones   cakes   foxes   kites   ropes   roses

nbeso _____ •   •

eitks _____ •   •

repos _____ •   •

kasec _____ •   •

xesof _____ •   •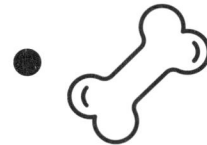

sseor _____ •   •

Better Together! Use this worksheet with week 22 of *Building Spelling Skills,* grade 1

Name _____

Maze of Blends

Help the ant get to the plant.
Follow the words that end with **nd** or **nt**.

cup · got · kind · ant · went · sent · mind · bend · find · want · mind · love · happy · bear · tiger · but · hat · wet · jam · sea · baby

134 · Spelling Games and Activities • EMC 8271 • © Evan-Moor Corporation

Better Together! Use this worksheet with week 22 of *Building Spelling Skills,* grade 1

Name _____

Clues and a Riddle

Read each clue and write a spelling word to answer it.

> ant   went   bend   find   mind   kind   sent   want

look for something and see it

nice

go last night

wish

what your knees do

Now write the letters from the gray boxes in order to solve the riddle.

I make you laugh and smile and cheer you up if you're sad,
I will always be there for you, even when you feel mad.

What am I?   I am a ☐ r ☐ ☐ ☐ ☐ .

Better Together! Use this worksheet with week 23 of *Building Spelling Skills*, grade 1

Name _____

Tennis Teammates

Read the team names.
Then read the word below each player.
Cut and glue each word below the correct team name.

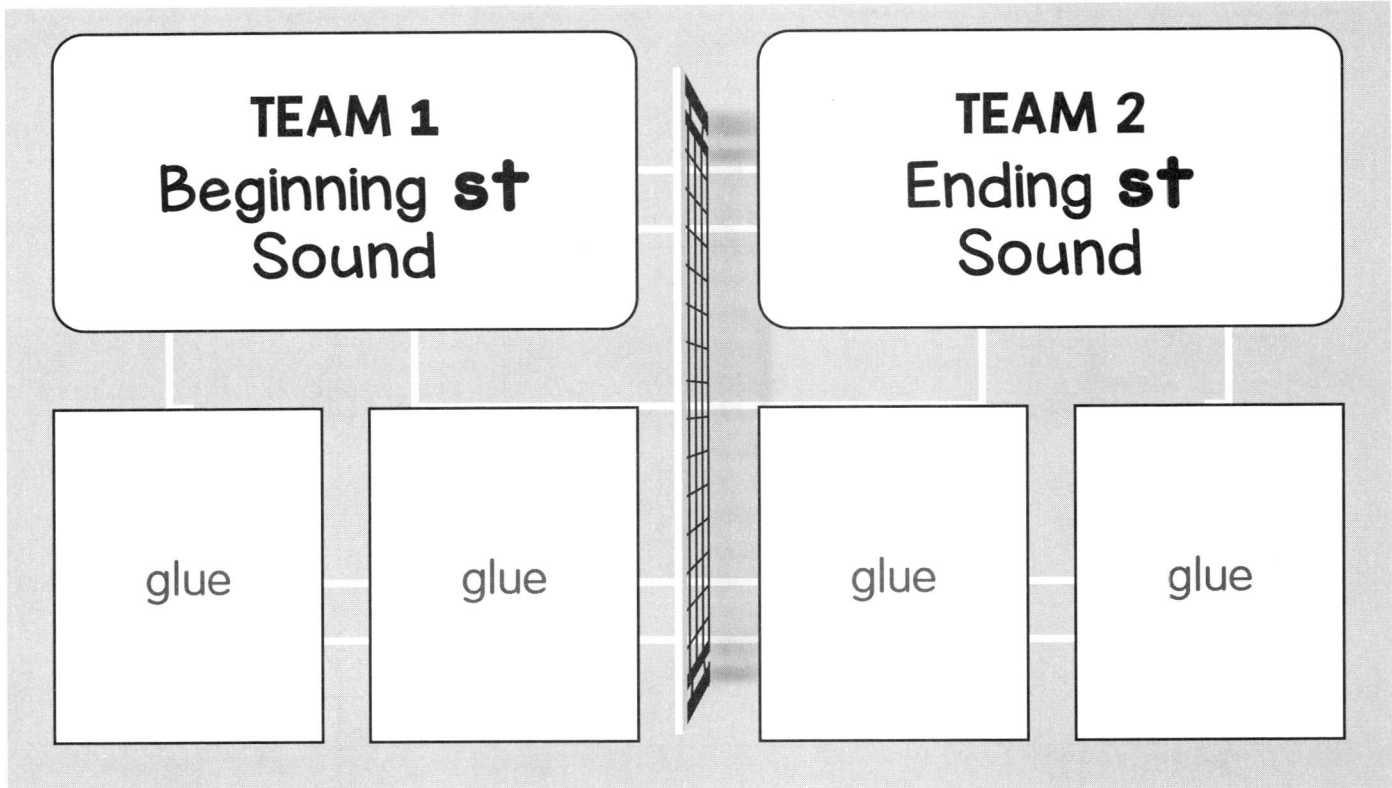

TEAM 1
Beginning **st** Sound

TEAM 2
Ending **st** Sound

glue   glue   glue   glue

nest   stamp   still   last

Better Together! Use this worksheet with week 23 of *Building Spelling Skills*, grade 1

Name _____

Missing at the Zoo

Write the missing letter to finish spelling the word.
Cross off each letter after you use it.

i   m   u   s   t   s

m___st

sta___p

mo___t

s___ep

st___ll

fa___t

fast   most   must   stamp   step   still

One More Drawing

Draw one more. Then write a word from the box that tells about the picture. Then add an **s** to the word you wrote.

> toad   boat   day   coat

_____

_____

_____

_____

Word Scramble

Unscramble the letters to write a word.
Then draw a line to match the word to a picture.

may stay play away

yalp _____ •

•

atys _____ •

•

waay _____ •

•

aym _____ •

•

Better Together! Use this worksheet with week 25 of *Building Spelling Skills*, grade 1

Name _____

Balls for All

The children want to play. But they only play with the balls with letters that spell the word below them.

Color the balls to spell the word below each child.

all

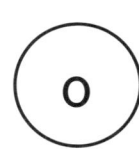    
o　k　a　l　l　l

wall

 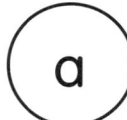    
w　a　l　l　i　t

will

 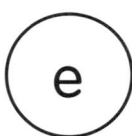    
h　e　w　i　l　l

tell

  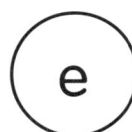   
d　t　e　l　l　a

Spelling Games and Activities • EMC 8271 • © Evan-Moor Corporation

Soccer Search

Find 4 words in the picture. Circle them.
Then write the words you found.

1. _____ _____ _____ _____

2. _____ _____ _____ _____

3. _____ _____ _____ _____ _____

4. _____ _____ _____ _____ _____

Grandma's House

Help the girl get to Grandma's house.
Write the words for each step.

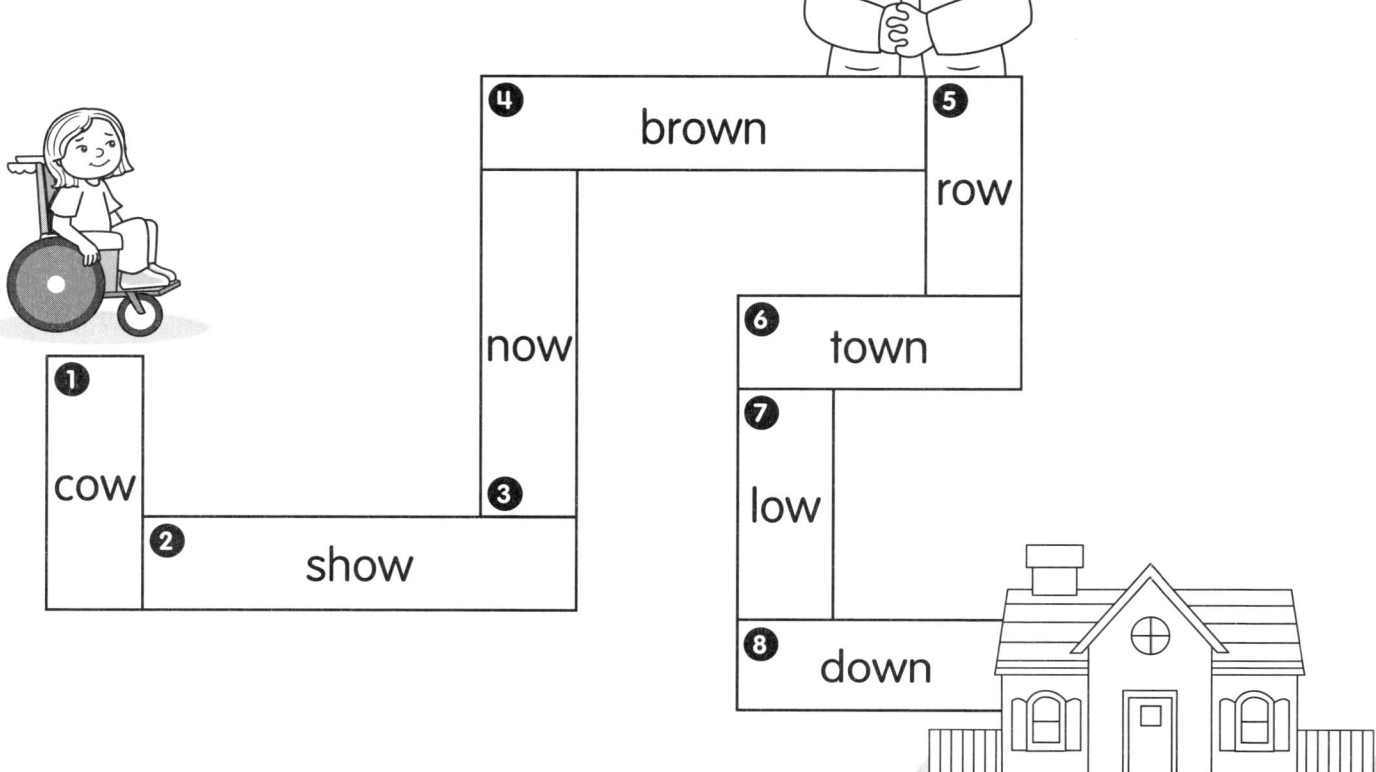

Step 1 ↓ cow

Step 2 → _____

Step 3 ↑ _____

Step 4 → _____

Step 5 ↓ _____

Step 6 ← _____

Step 7 ↓ _____

Step 8 → _____

Unscramble and Solve

Unscramble the letters to write a word from the box.

> town   cow   brown   down

woc ___ ___ ___
         1

ronbw ___ ___ ___ ___ ___
            2   4

dnwo ___ ___ ___ ___
              3

nowt ___ ___ ___ ___
                     5

Now write the numbered letters in the matching spaces to answer the riddle.

What does a king wear on his head?

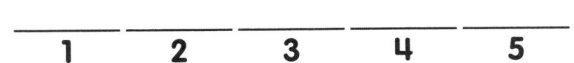
1   2   3   4   5

Better Together! Use this worksheet with week 27 of *Building Spelling Skills*, grade 1

Name _____

Tractors

Write the missing letter to spell the word. Then draw a line to each letter to spell the word and get to the barn. The first line has been drawn.

car   are   jar

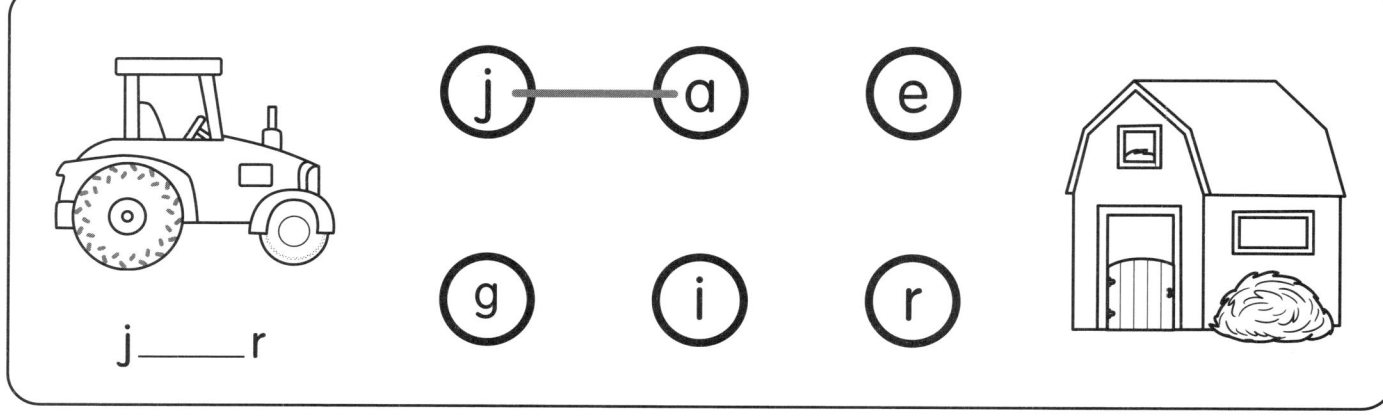

j____r

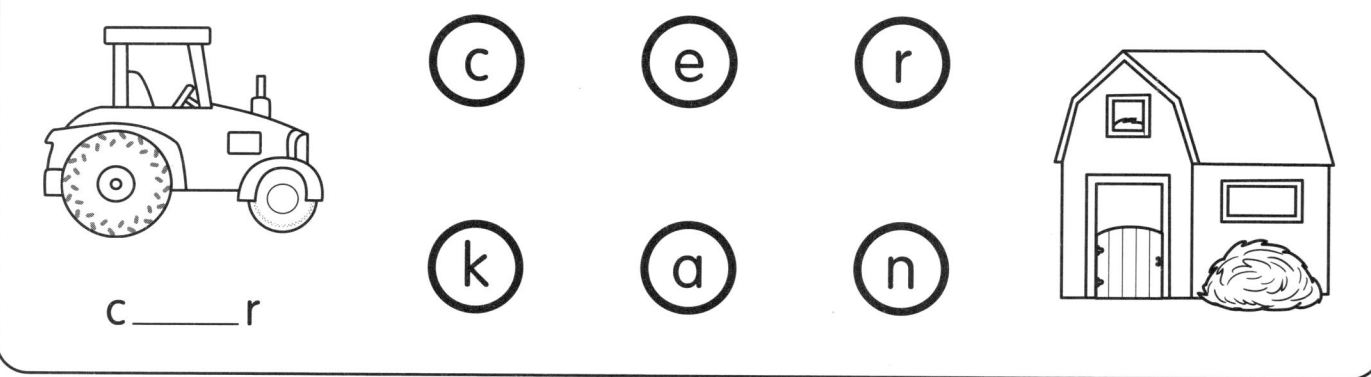

c____r

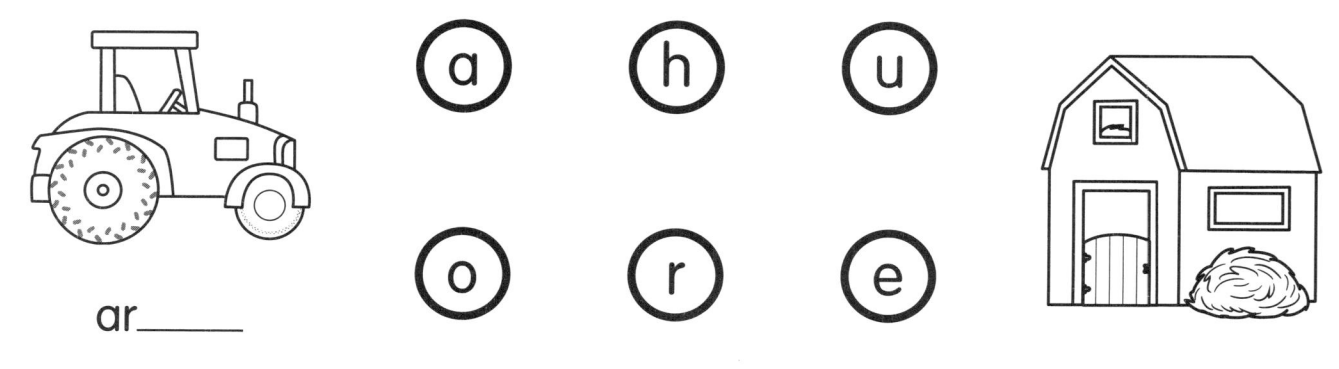

ar____

Barn on the Farm

Help put the animals in the barn.
Cut and glue the animals onto the correct barn.

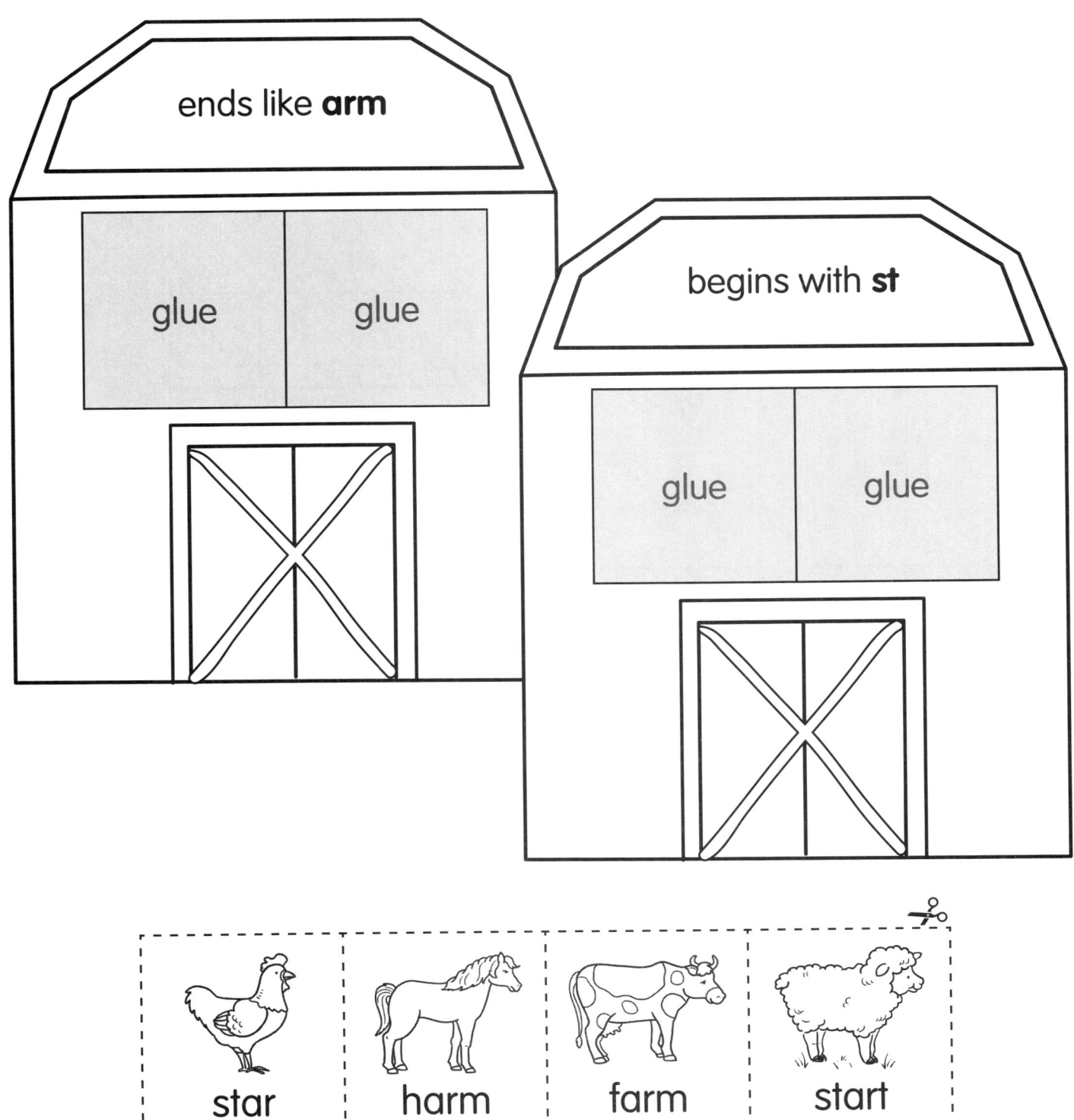

Better Together! Use this worksheet with week 28 of *Building Spelling Skills*, grade 1

Name _____

Animal Treats

Help each animal get a treat by following a spelling word. Color the squares to spell a word. Look at the example.

bunny

b	u	m
e	n	n
e	v	y

START → END

kitten

t	a	k
t	t	i
e	n	i

← START   END

little

l	i	t
e	a	t
d	e	l

START → END

puppy

b	u	p
i	p	b
e	p	y

← START   END

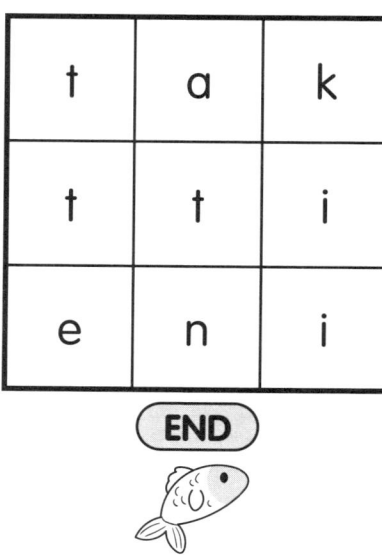
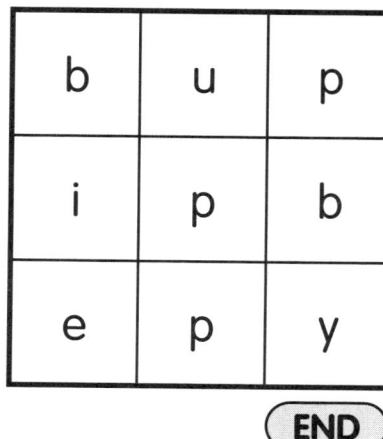

146   Spelling Games and Activities • EMC 8271 • © Evan-Moor Corporation

Better Together! Use this worksheet with week 28 of *Building Spelling Skills*, grade 1

Name _____

Secret Sentences

Use the secret code to write a spelling word. Match each shape in the word to a letter.

⊙	■	✿	♥	◆	○
a	e	f	h	i	l
☽	△	🎀	★	〰	☀
m	n	p	t	u	y

Example

You are __f__ __u__ __n__ __n__ __y__ !
   ✿ 〰 △ △ ☀

Can I have a __p__ __e__ __n__ __n__ __y__ ?
   🎀 ■ △ △ ☀

I feel __h__ __a__ __p__ __p__ __y__ .
   ♥ ⊙ 🎀 🎀 ☀

Where is my __m__ __i__ __t__ __t__ __e__ __n__ ?
   ☽ ◆ ★ ★ ■ △

I see a __l__ __i__ __t__ __t__ __l__ __e__ bird.
   ○ ◆ ★ ★ ○ ■

Better Together! Use this worksheet with week 29 of *Building Spelling Skills*, grade 1

Name _____

Baseball Teams

Read the flags.
Then read the words below each player.
Cut and glue each word below the correct flag.

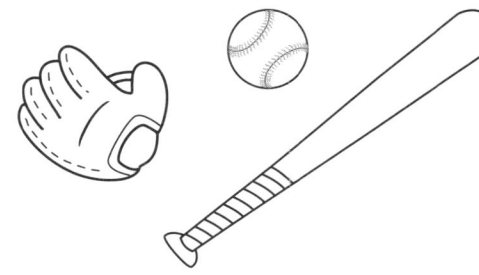

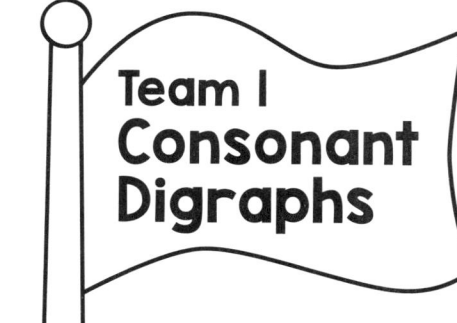

Team 1
Consonant
Digraphs

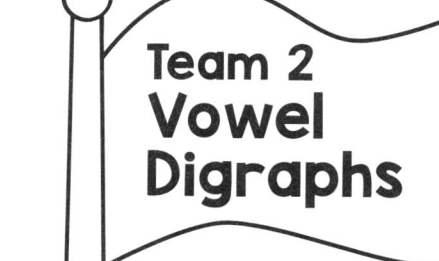

Team 2
Vowel
Digraphs

| glue | glue | glue | glue |

saw

then

lawn

what

Missing in the Forest

Write the missing letter to finish spelling the word.
Cross off each letter after you use it.

Picture This!

Finish the sentence about the picture using the words from the box.
Use each word one time.

> book   look   wood   took   good   take   stood   stand

We _____ and _____ a bow.

I read a _____ _____.

She _____ up and _____ a cookie.

_____ at the man chop the _____.

Better Together! Use this worksheet with week 30 of *Building Spelling Skills*, grade 1

Name _____

Missing in Space

Write the missing letters to finish spelling the word.
Color the creatures who have the missing letters.

| take | took | stand | stood |

st_____d

 o
 a
 u
 o

t___k___

 y
 c
 a
 e

sta_____

 m
 n
 d
 b

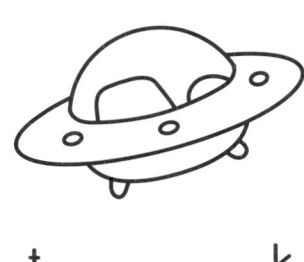
t_____k

 o
 u
 o
 h

© Evan-Moor Corporation • EMC 8271 • Spelling Games and Activities

Spelling Strategies
How to Spell Hard Words

There are so many words!
When you don't know one, use these ways to spell it.

👂✋	**Say the word.** Listen to the sounds. Count the syllables. **Ask yourself** What do I hear? What do I know?
Silent e makes a vowel say its name.	**Think about rules.** **Ask yourself** What rule can I use?
-ell family bell fell sell tell well yell	**Think about words that you can spell.** **Ask yourself** Is it part of a word family?
jel|ly|fish	**Break up the word into parts.** Break compound words into two words. Break words into syllables. **Ask yourself** Can I break it into smaller parts?

152   Spelling Games and Activities • EMC 8271 • © Evan-Moor Corporation

Spelling Strategies
Spell Vowel Sounds

All words have vowel sounds. Some are short. Some are long. Some are different. What sound do you hear?

Short Vowels

Write the letter you hear.

c**a**t, f**e**d, h**i**ll, t**o**p, r**u**n

Or write a vowel team.

l**au**gh, s**aw**

Long Vowels

Write the letter you hear.

b**a**ke, m**e**, **i**ce, n**o**te, **u**se

Or write a vowel team.

pl**ay**, s**ea**, sh**ee**p, fr**ie**d, b**oa**t, fr**ui**t, y**ou**

oo Sounds

The pair **oo** has its own sound.

c**oo**k, g**oo**d, l**oo**k, st**oo**d, t**oo**k, w**oo**d

It can also sound like long **u**.

b**oo**th, f**oo**d, l**oo**se, sc**oo**p, t**oo**th

ow Sounds

The pair **ow** has its own sound.

br**ow**n, d**ow**n, fl**ow**er, n**ow**, t**ow**n

It can also sound like long **o**.

l**ow**, rainb**ow**, r**ow**, sh**ow**

Spelling Strategies

Spell Consonant Sounds— Singles and Blends

Most consonants have one sound. **C** has two sounds. Some consonants are used in teams. You hear both sounds. What sound do you hear?

One Sound

These letters have one sound.

bus, **d**ig, **f**eet, **h**ide, **j**ar, **k**ind, **l**et, **m**ay, **n**ow, **p**et, **q**uack, **r**ed, **t**en, **v**ery, **w**ill, fi**x**, **z**ip

Consonant Teams

Some consonants are used in a team. No vowel is in between.

brown, **cr**ab, **dr**agon, **fr**uit, **gr**ass, **pr**ize, **tr**ee, **cl**oud, **fl**oss, **pl**ay, **sl**ice, **sc**ared, **sm**all, **sn**ake, **sp**in, **st**ar

S or Soft C?

When you hear an **s** sound, write an **s** most of the time.

sat, **s**ob, **s**un, **s**tep, u**s**

Write a **c** before an **e** or an **i**.

jui**ce**, **ci**ty

K or Hard C?

When you hear a **k** sound, write a **c** most of the time.

car, **c**ow, **c**ut, **c**rab, o**c**topus

Write a **k** before an **e** or an **i**. Write a **k** at the end.

keep, **ki**te, boo**k**

Spelling Strategies

Spell Consonant Sounds— Digraphs

Some consonant teams make a different sound. What sound do you hear?

ck Sound

The **ck** team makes a **k** sound.

ba**ck**, pa**ck**, ja**ck**et

sh Sound

The **sh** team makes its own sound.

sharp, **sh**ell, bru**sh**, di**sh**

th Sound

The **th** team makes its own sound.

mou**th**, too**th**, **th**e, **th**is

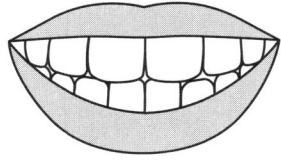

wh Sound

The **wh** team makes its own sound.

what, **wh**ale, **wh**eel

© Evan-Moor Corporation • EMC 8271 • Spelling Games and Activities

Spelling Strategies
Break Down Words— Compounds

Compound words are two short words put together.

Break down a compound word.

1. Say the word.

2. Find the two short words in it. Write them.

butter

fly

3. Write the compound word.

butterfly

Spelling Strategies

Break Down Words— Syllables

Syllables are short parts of a word. When you say a syllable, your chin moves.

Break a word into syllables.

1. Say the word.

   umbrella

2. Listen to each syllable. Write the sounds.

   um   brel   la

3. Write the syllables together.

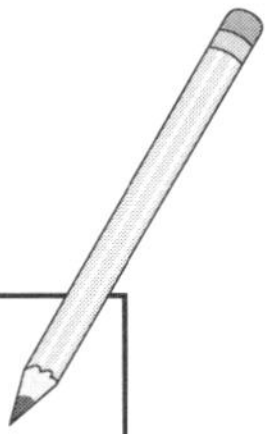

   umbrella

Answer Key

Page 12

Page 13

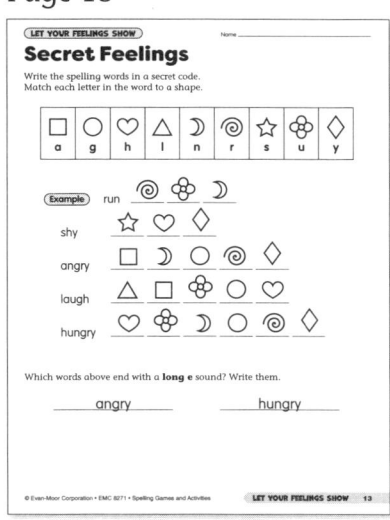

Page 14

Page 15

Page 16

Page 17

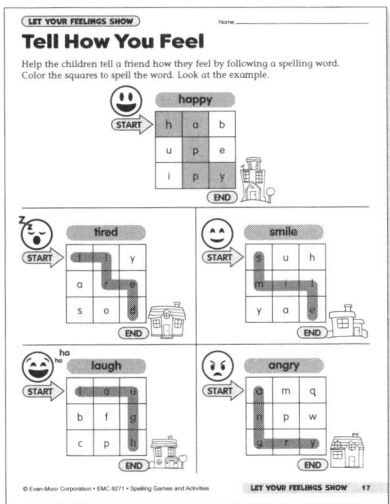

Page 22
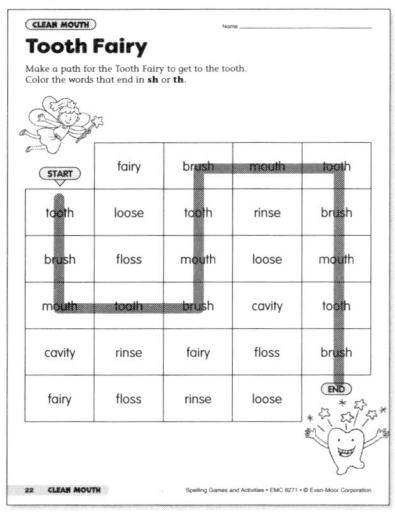

Page 23
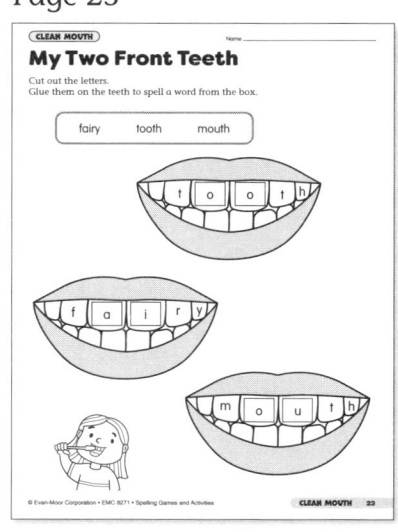

Page 24

Page 25
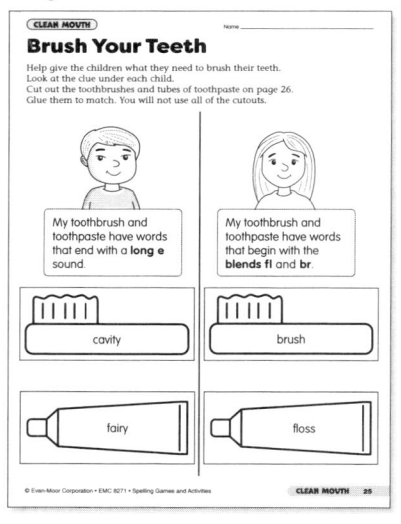

Page 27
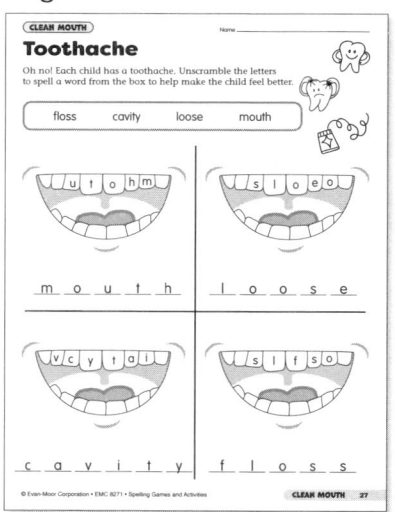

Page 32
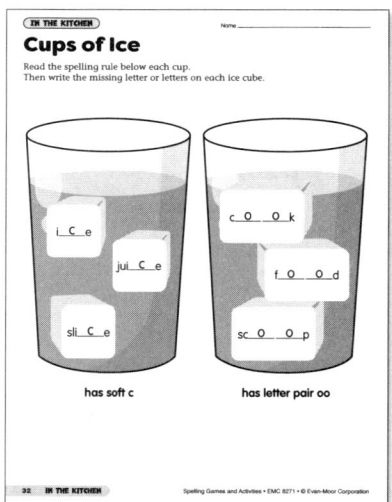

Page 33

Page 34

Page 35
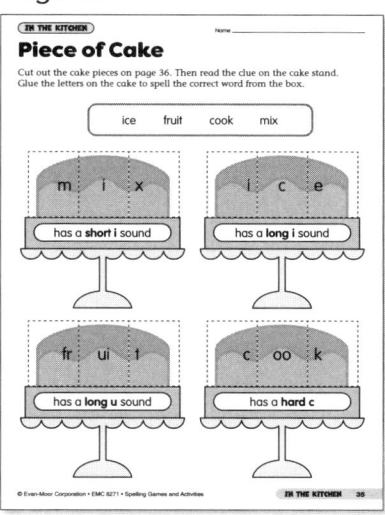

Page 37
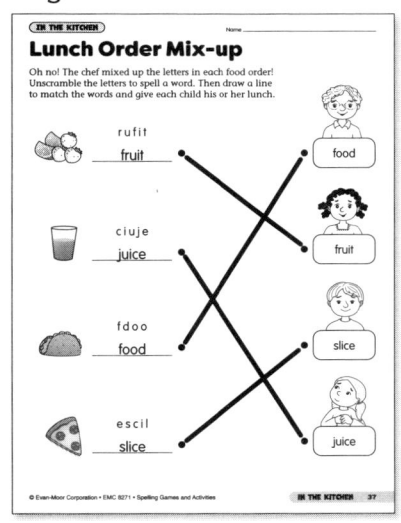

Page 42

Page 43
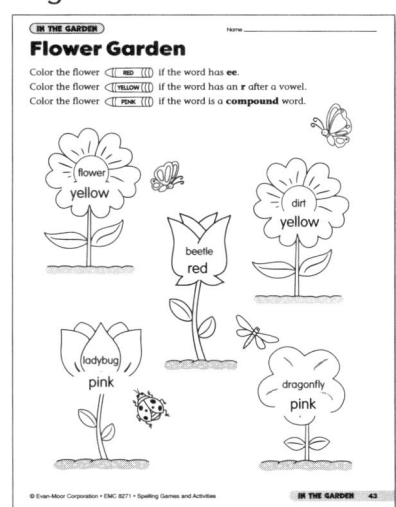

Page 44
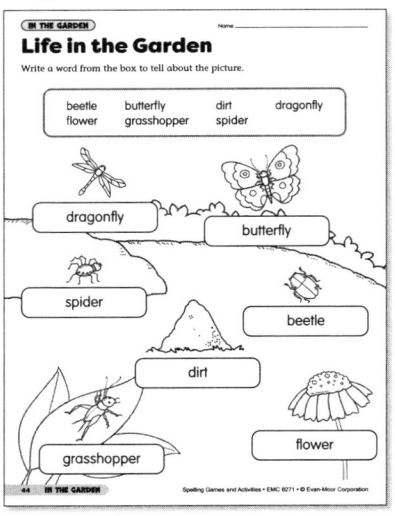

Page 45

Page 46
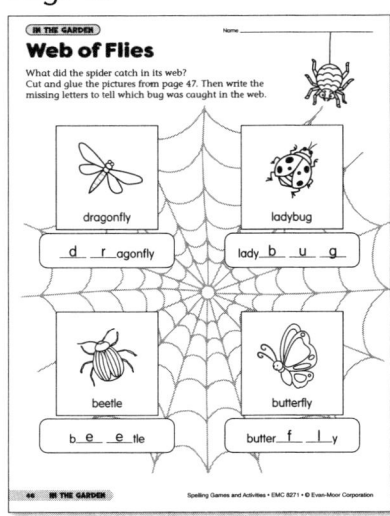

Page 52
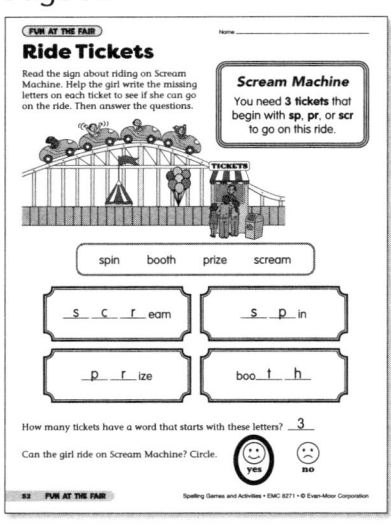

Page 53
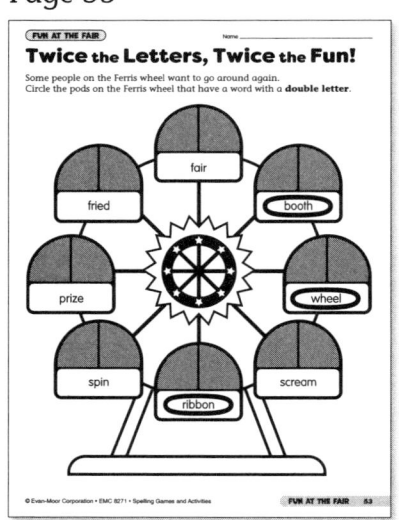

Page 54
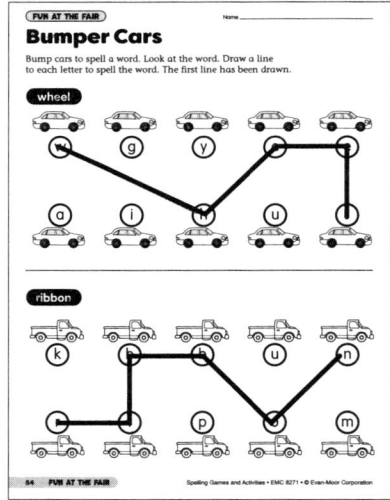

Page 55

Page 56

Page 57
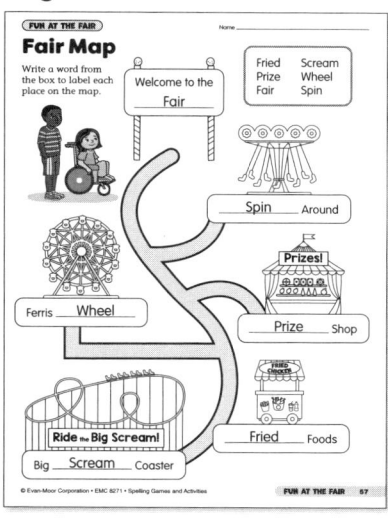

Page 62
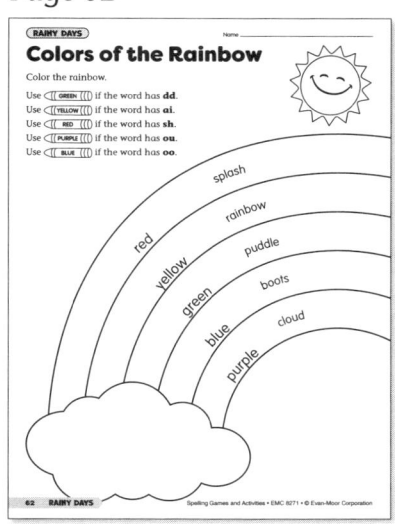

Page 63
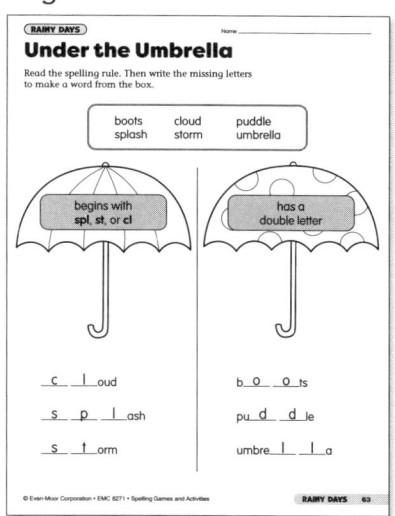

Page 64
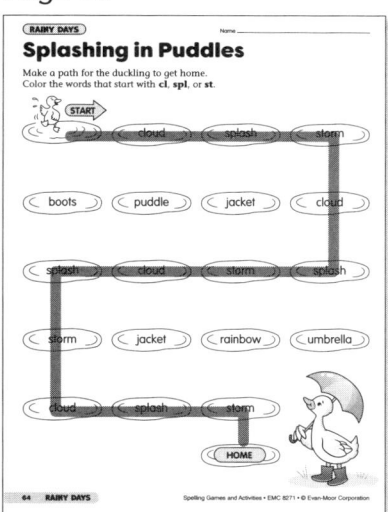

© Evan-Moor Corporation • EMC 8271 • Spelling Games and Activities

Page 65

Page 66

Page 67

Page 72
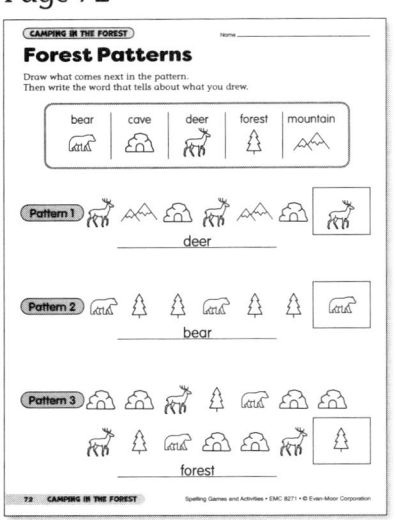

Page 73
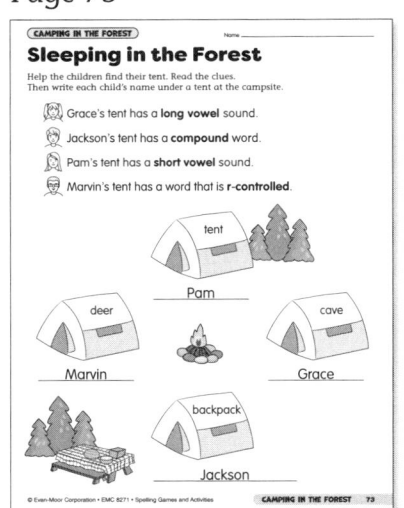

Page 74
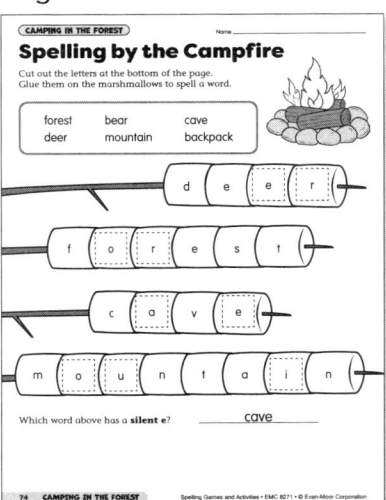

Page 75
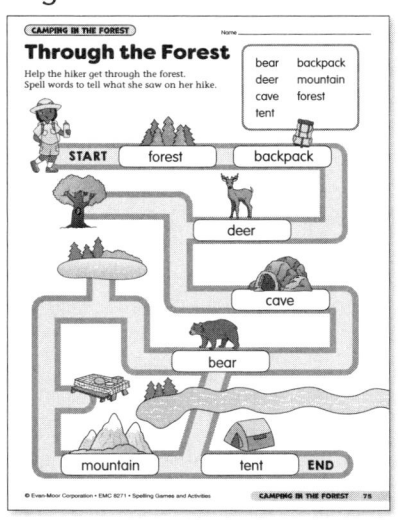

Page 76

Page 82
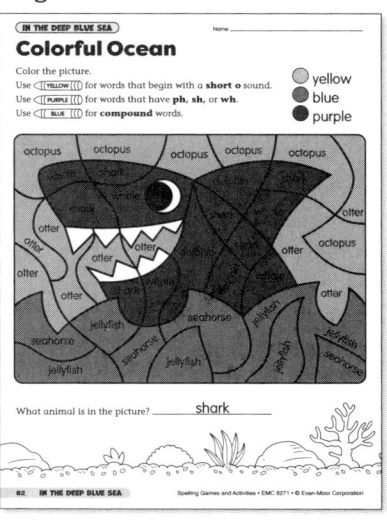

Page 83

Page 84

Page 85
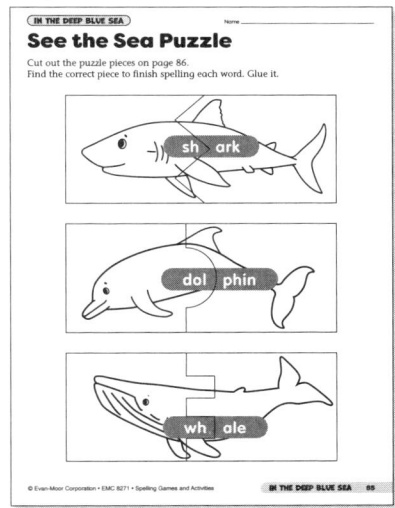

© Evan-Moor Corporation • EMC 8271 • Spelling Games and Activities

Page 87
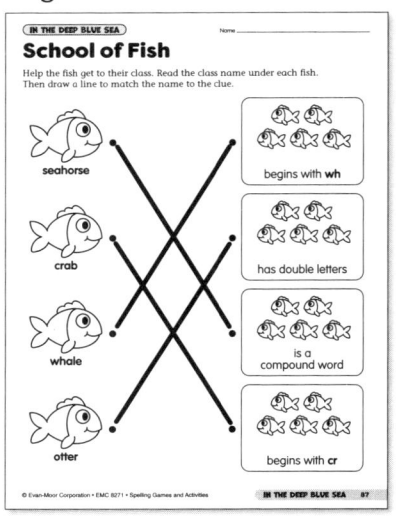

Page 92
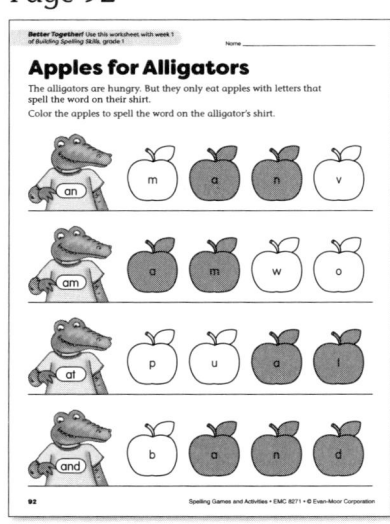

Page 93

Page 94

Page 95
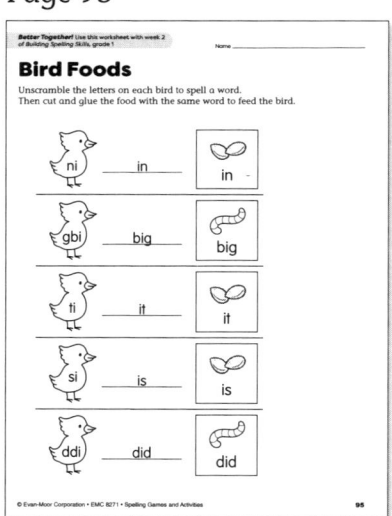

Page 96

Page 97

Page 98
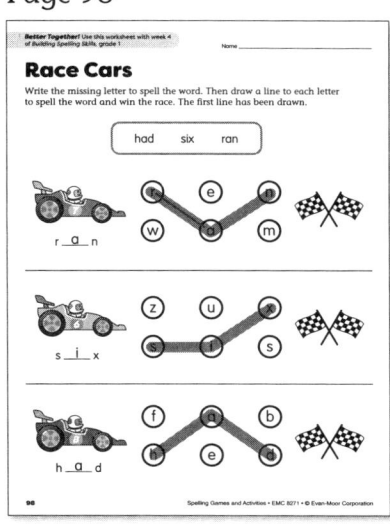

Page 99
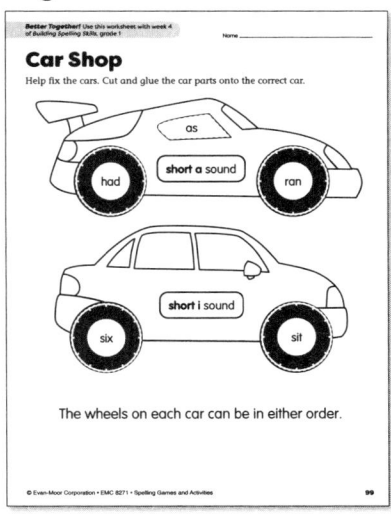

Page 100

Page 101
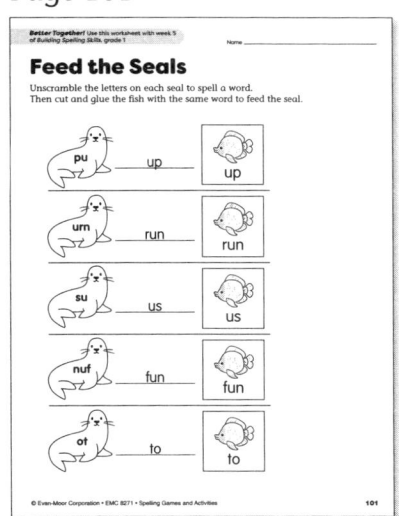

Page 102

Page 103

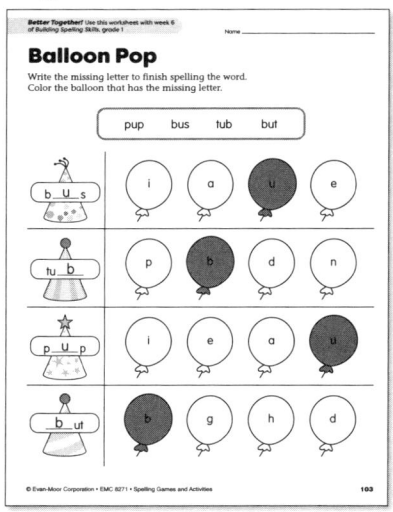

Page 104

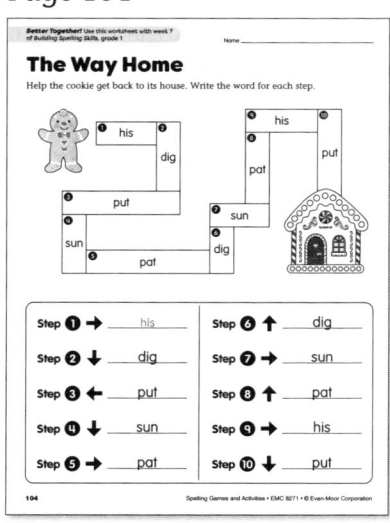

Page 105

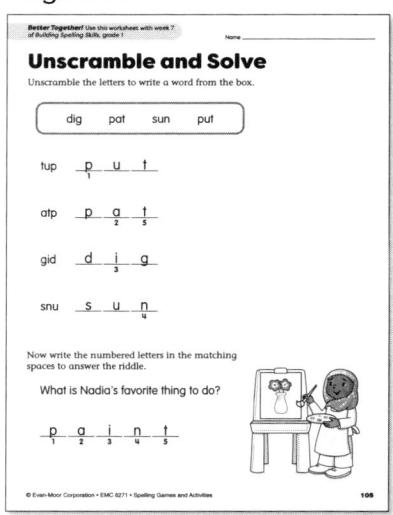

Page 106

Page 107

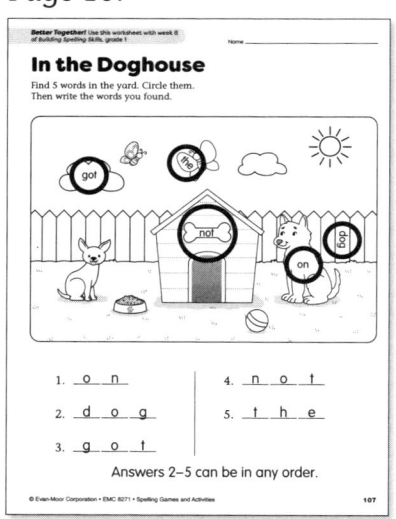

Page 108

Page 109

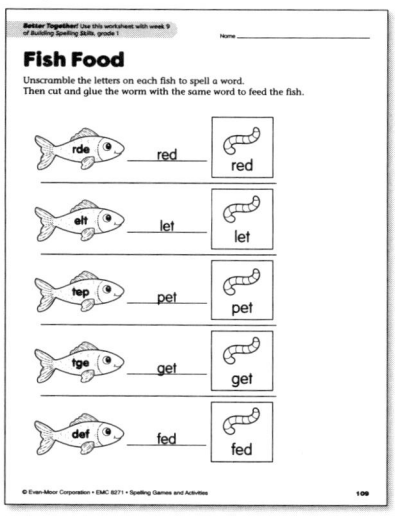

Page 110

Page 111

Page 112

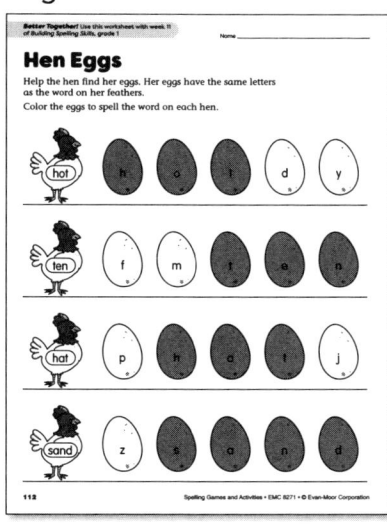

Page 113

Page 114

Page 115
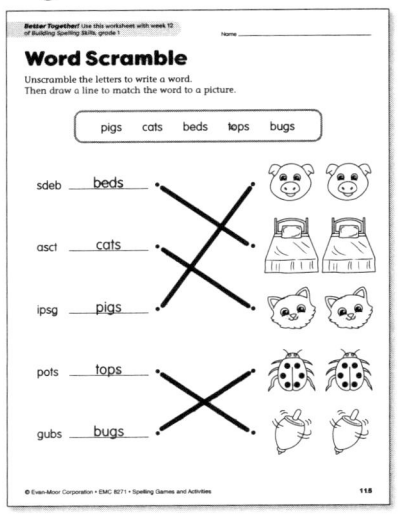

Page 116
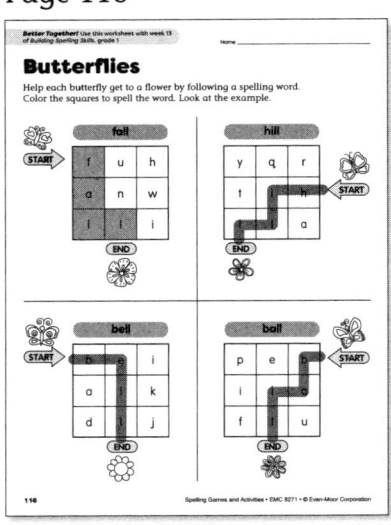

Page 117

Page 118

Page 119
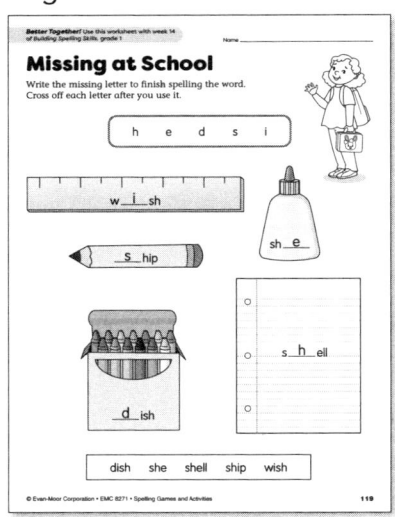

Page 120
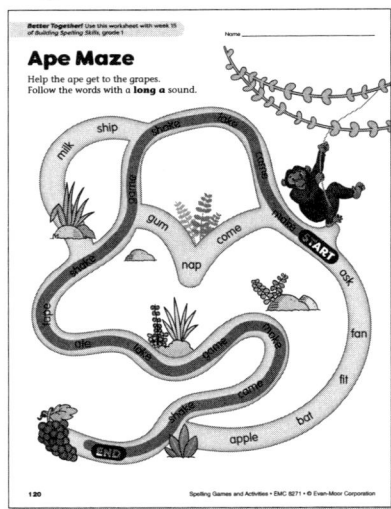

Page 121
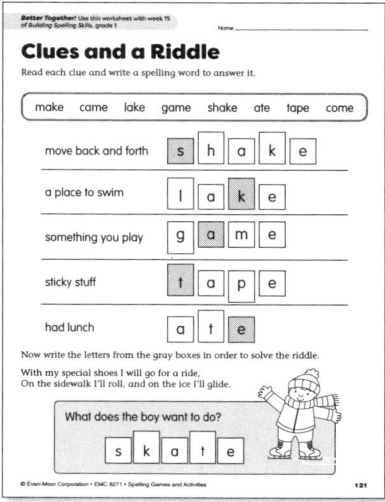

Page 122
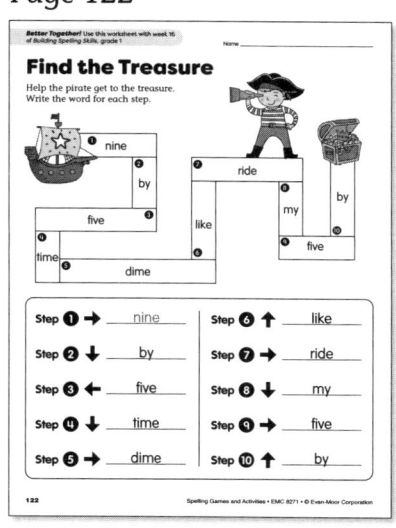

Page 123
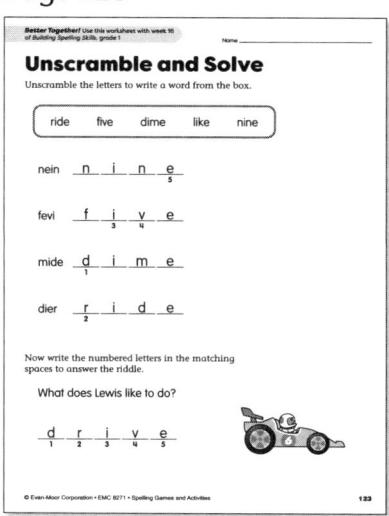

Page 124
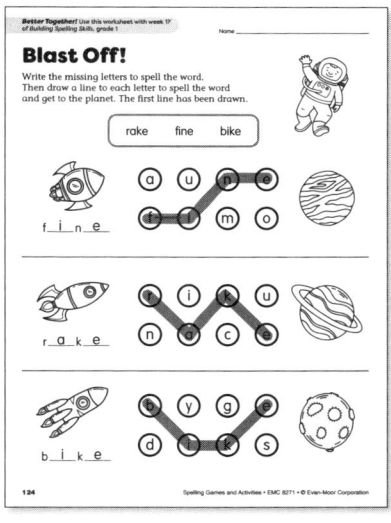

Page 125

Page 126

Page 127
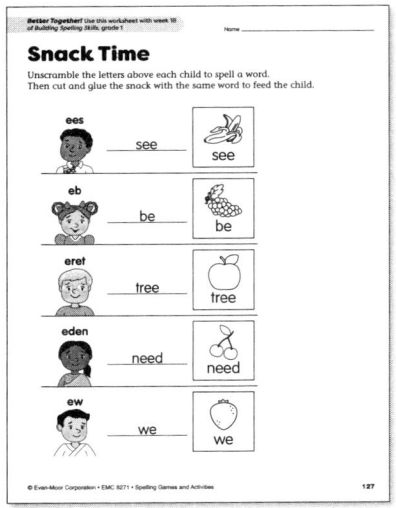

Page 128
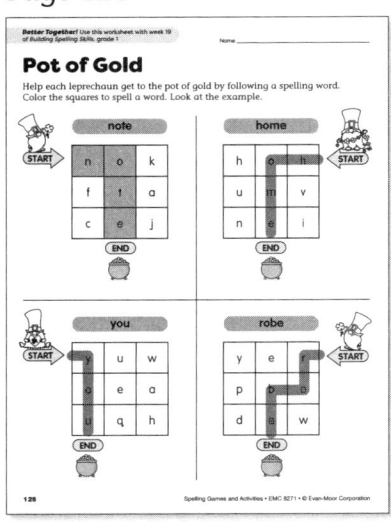

Page 129
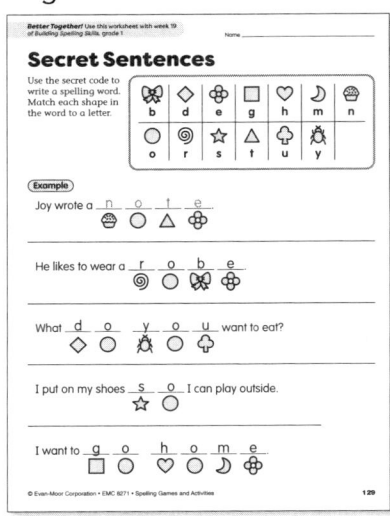

Page 130
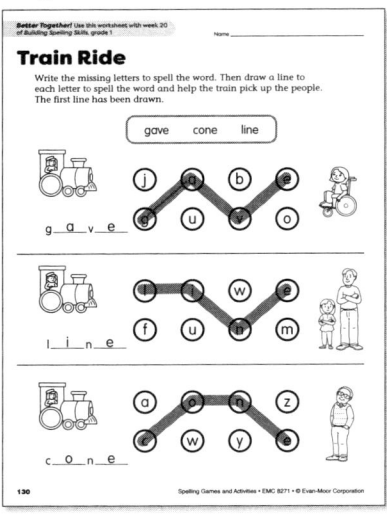

Page 131
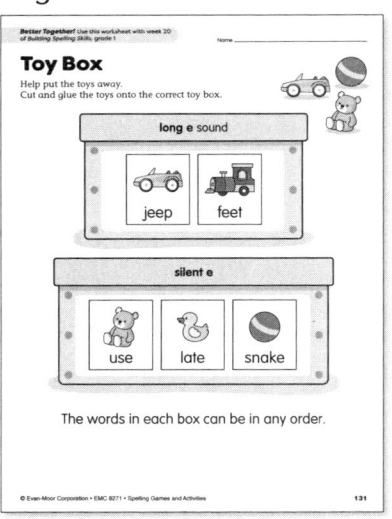

Page 132

Page 133
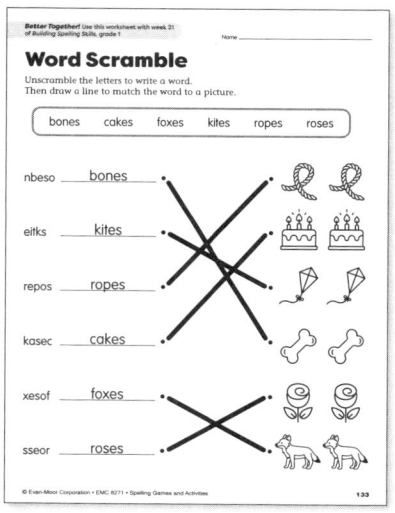

Page 134
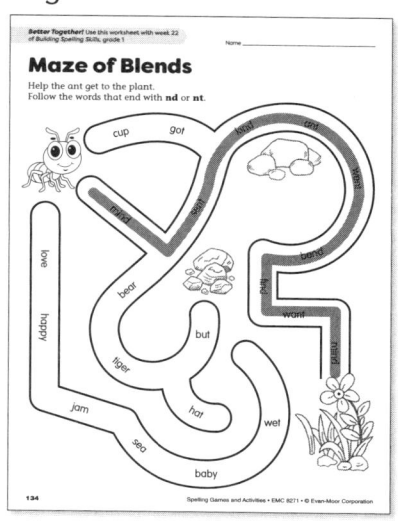

Page 135
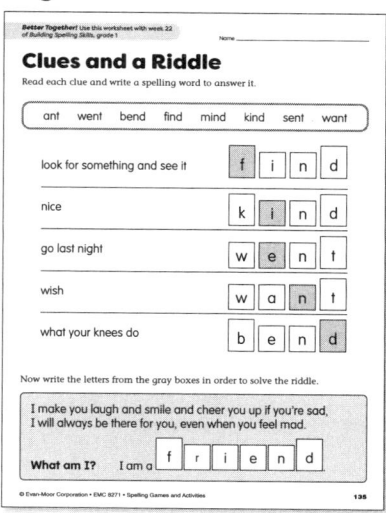

Page 136
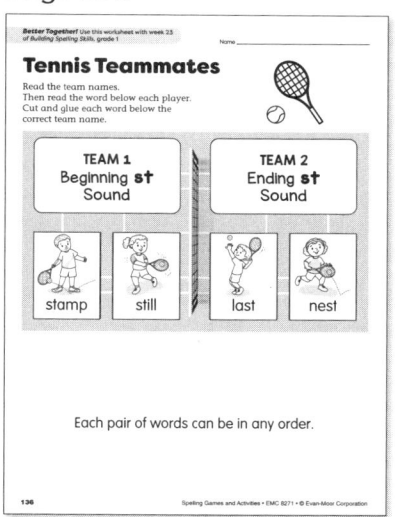

Page 137

Page 138
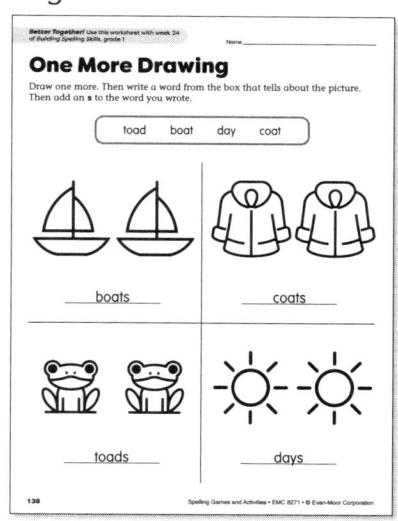

Page 139
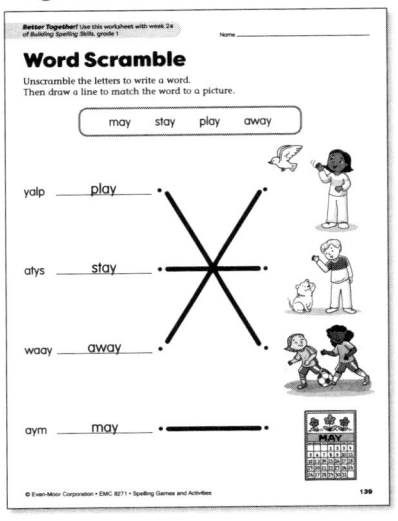

Page 140
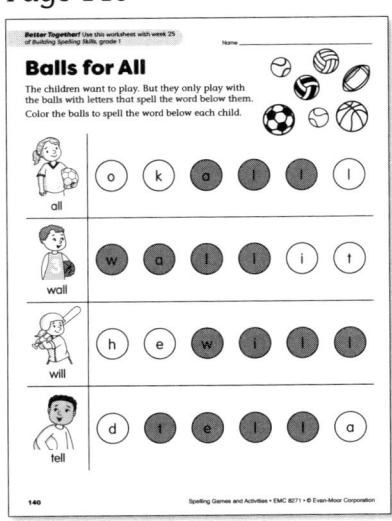

Page 141
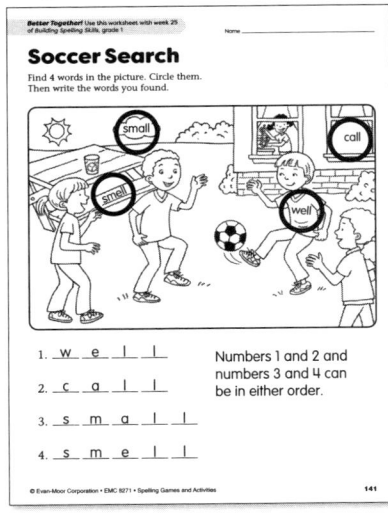

Page 142
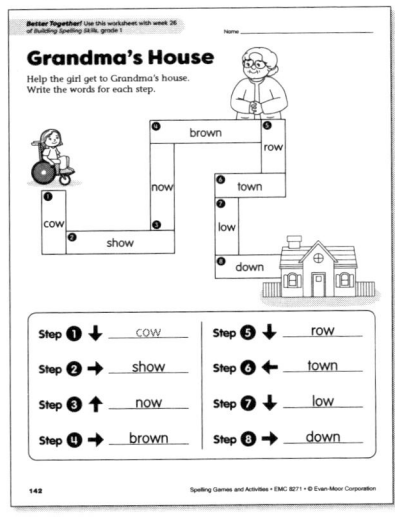

Page 143
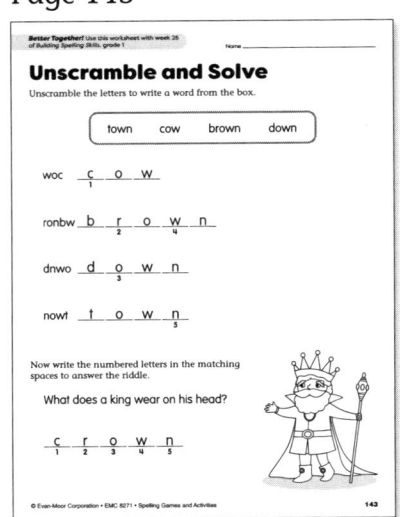

Page 144
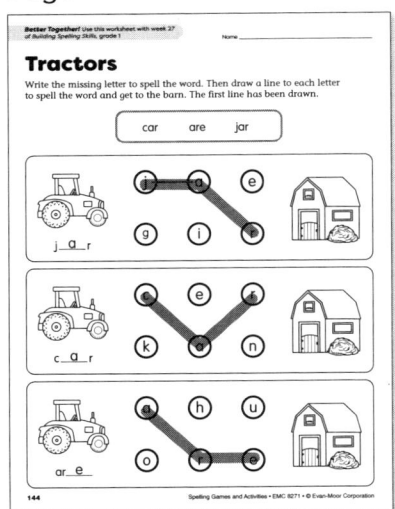

Page 145

Page 146

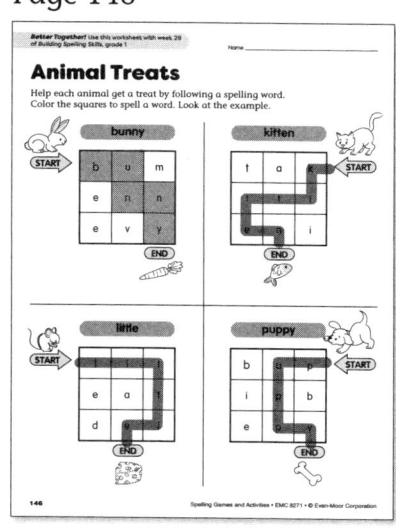

Page 147

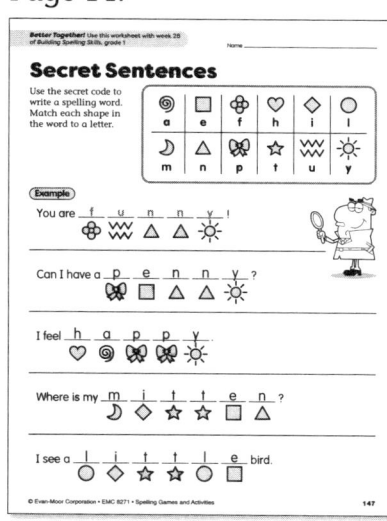

Page 148

Page 149

Page 150

Page 151